The author is about to embark on his fourth Lions tour. He was born and brought up in North Wales and now lives in rural Cheshire. He works part time and volunteers for a charity. He is married to his travelling companion Lisa. Iain has two grown up daughters and a grandson aged eight years. When not writing, he enjoys golf, gardening, science and music.

Dedication

This book took eleven years to complete. I had the initial idea before the 2005 New Zealand tour, took some notes on that tour and then started writing in earnest in 2006. It is dedicated to Alfred Shaw and Arthur Shrewsbury who first came up with the idea and arranged the first tour. It is also dedicated to everyone who has ever set foot on a ship or plane to support the team of these Great Islands of ours, and lastly to the players who place their bodies on the line for our benefit and the perpetuation of the great institution that is the British and Irish Lions.

Iain Richard James Goodwin

Travel Lions

AUSTIN MACAULEY
PUBLISHERS LTD.

Copyright © Iain Goodwin (2017)

The right of Iain Goodwin to be identified as author of this work has been asserted by him in accordance with section 77 and 78 of the Copyright, Designs and Patents Act 1988.

All rights reserved. No part of this publication may be reproduced, stored in a retrieval system, or transmitted in any form or by any means, electronic, mechanical, photocopying, recording, or otherwise, without the prior permission of the publishers.

Any person who commits any unauthorized act in relation to this publication may be liable to criminal prosecution and civil claims for damages.

A CIP catalogue record for this title is available from the British Library.

ISBN 9781786934765 (Paperback)
ISBN 9781786934772 (E-Book)
www.austinmacauley.com

First Published (2017)
Austin Macauley Publishers Ltd.
25 Canada Square
Canary Wharf
London
E14 5LQ

Acknowledgments

This book would not have been possible without the support of my wife Lisa, and guidance from Rob Appleton (an author published by Austin Macauley). I dedicate it to everyone who ever played for the Lions and the thousands of supporters in the friendliest invading army in history. 25% of all profits from this book will be donated to St Luke's Hospice, Winterley.

Chapter 1
Early memories

I remember seeing a grainy black and white photograph during a summer's day in my childhood, it was on the back of a newspaper, now long re-cycled. The picture was of a man gliding, as if moving through the air and not running on the ground, with a rugby ball in two hands as if daring anyone to take it from him. The man was wearing a shirt with a badge on the left-hand side that I could not make out, the picture was mesmerising, and I stared at it for what seemed to be an eternity, I can clearly see it in my minds' eye now.

The photograph was of the great Welsh fly half, Barry John in a 1971 Test Match in New Zealand playing the legendary All Blacks. So began my fascination with the Lions. They famously won that series under the leadership of the legendary Willie John McBride. Most of that team played the All Blacks again in Cardiff in 1973, and beat them again, and of course that team's core went down in Rugby legend as the 'Invincibles' after the South African tour of 1974. On this tour another Welsh fly half, Phil Bennett, became a legend.

A British rugby Union team first made an appearance in 1888, when sporting entrepreneurs Alfred Shaw and Arthur Shrewsbury, took a team to New Zealand and Australia. It was an unofficial tour as such.

Alfred Shaw was an ex-cricketer turned entrepreneur. Arthur Shrewsbury a cricketer, who, it is said, vied with WG for the honour of being the best batsman of his times. He was also a rugby administrator. The players were selected from England, Scotland and Wales.

The tour captain, Bob Seddon of Swinton and Lancashire, tragically drowned while sculling on the Hunter River after a game at Maitland, New South Wales. Andrew Stoddart, who had captained the England cricket team on eight occasions, took over the helm. The tour began appropriately in New Zealand, and the tourists played nine games winning six, losing two and drawing one. They moved on to Australia where they won fourteen of sixteen matches, drawing the other two. A number of these games, in keeping with the financial aim of the tour were played as 'Aussie rules'. The tour was concluded with an unbeaten return to New Zealand for the final 10 matches.

The first official tour, involving all of the home unions, was to South Africa in 1910.

Another 'combined British team' also toured to Argentina in the same year. The tour to South Africa being far less successful than the one to Argentina, who at that time were relative novices when it came to Test match rugby. The first world war caused a gap of twelve years before the next tour, again to South Africa.

The Lions name was coined during the inter-war period, when the emblem on the players' jersey and lapel badges gave them their alternative title.

The Lions had won series in Argentina (1927, 1936), had changed their shirts from navy blue to red. In 1950 in New Zealand, although losing the series they had introduced the world to the kind of open rugby which has become their hallmark. In the same year, they had won the series against Australia 2 – 0. They shared a series with the Springboks 2 – 2 in 1955, with Wales stand-off Cliff Morgan, England's late great Dickie Jeeps, and Ireland wing Tony O'Reilly, mesmerising the Springboks.

In 1959 they registered series wins against Australia and Canada but suffered another series defeat against the All Blacks. One series win in 1966 against Australia would follow, albeit this, as were the tours against Canada and Argentina, was merely a side show before the big tests against the All Blacks and the Springboks.

1971 and 1974 were of course the big years for the Lions who then had a pretty fallow time of it for fifteen years.

In 1989 the Lions arrived in Australia for the first tour where the hosts were no longer a tour side show.

The Australians had of course completed a Grand Slam in 1984 and were by now more than worthy of Lions star billing. In a little over two years they would be World Champions. Sir Ian McGeechan, an 'Invincible' with an obvious excellent Lions pedigree was coach for this tour which would continue his trip into Lions folklore. The tour was won by the Lions 2 – 1 in a very physical series, the foundations of what we all now recognise as the Lions loop were laid.

1993 in New Zealand was a near miss for the Lions, losing the decider and series 2 – 1. So it was onto the World Champions, South Africa in 1997, where we were given no chance, and where the fanatical Lions support could be seen to be growing... considerably.

The tour was of course famously won 2 – 1, and I feel it was here that the current huge interest in touring with the Lions commenced. This of course coincided with the tour being televised by Sky for the first time, BBC another jewel escapes your grasp.

So, for all of you with those tatty Scottish Provident shirts still in the wardrobe many thanks from a generation of Lions fans. That is of course not to forget the many thousands who toured in series well before this, when it was not quite the phenomenon it is now.

Chapter 2

Now there is an idea

The only real reason that we have travelled at these particular times to these particular places is to watch the Lions. We may have gone otherwise but these trips were planned specifically around attendance at the tests. A book of our experiences seems to me to be a natural progression from that idea.

The 2001 tour to Australia saw early starts for those of us who stayed at home, it again saw a huge swell in travelling support. I watched all three tests in our local pub, where a full cooked and a pint seemed to be the order of the day. It was of course heart breaking to have lost that last test when it seemed to be in our control, but a loss it was and we had to stomach it, along with pints of beer accompanied by sausage, egg, bacon, fried bread and beans. What is it about a full breakfast that we find so attractive? I can't tell the difference between a full English, full Scottish, full Irish or full Welsh. I have had them all and with the exception of white pudding, black pudding, haggis or rarebit they are all basically the same.

Back to the tour. I knew that friends of my landlord, Danny Jones had gone on the Tour but at that time I did not know any of them. So, it was that on a summers evening in the Hawk pub in Haslington, South Cheshire, a certain Mr Andrew Mason esquire strolled in wearing his Lions 2001 top, having just returned from that tour. He regaled us of many tales from the tour, some which could be published, some which could not, or could as long as they were wrapped in brown paper bags. Over the coming weeks, it became apparent that a further tour was planned in 2005 to New Zealand. I knew then that my Lions time was approaching and that I had to be part of that tour. The thought of seeing the Lions facing up to the Haka seemed to me to be the ultimate in rugby.

Mr John Stubbs, organiser extraordinaire would again lead Sandbach Rugby Club on this tour. I had long since decided that I was going and also that I would take in the potentially pivotal second test rather than all three in order to see as much of the countries in between as I could with my then partner now wife, Lisa. The reason for going remained the same, to see the Lions.

Of course to see the Lions you need tickets.

Many of you will have been to Wimbledon, who in my opinion have one of the fairest ticketing systems in operation. For those of you who don't know you basically apply to go in a ballot and if successful you get tickets to one of the show courts. You can of course queue. I have been in the ballot on three occasions and have had Court 1, Centre Court, and the Men's Final (Federer v Nadal). For god sake I have even had Ryder Cup tickets and other Rugby tickets by following similar principles. The point that I am making here is that we all should have the chance to attend by ballot or queue up. This is not the case with the Lions as I was to discover in 2005, and it is the one thing in the whole process that makes me, and many others, want to scream.

Basically, on this occasion I looked to join a ballot or a queue to see if I could get two tickets. The one answer I got, and many of you will have had the same one, was 'the only way to get tickets is by going on an official tour'. Now these official tours are all very well, but they hold a couple of problems for me;

1. You have to go where they say.
2. They generally take you to only one country.
3. They are prohibitively expensive certainly in the case of New Zealand (2005) at least £4,500 per person.
4. It opens up a huge black market in ticket sales to fans who don't want to be subject to 1, 2 or 3.

In my view, absolutely fine for people who want to do that sort of thing, however there are many of us who don't want to do 1 or 2 and can't afford the price. So why then are there not a set amount of tickets for the test matches to queue up, or enter a ballot for? Well I can assure you that I asked this question of the Lions HQ, the RFU, the IRB, the NZRFU, the Ministry for Culture and Sport and did not find any acceptable answer. So my chance at tickets from this avenue were limited to say the least. Next I became aware that New Zealand residents had a ballot in Operation and fortunately I had a friend who was resident in New Zealand.

Enter Trevor Palin, ex–Haslingtonian, airline pilot and sometime golfer, who heroically entered the ballot on my behalf but could only get the Auckland midweek game, which was before the third test and after I had left New Zealand; a great effort nonetheless. Stubby meanwhile had been trying on my behalf and, like the arch deliverer he is, got me two at four times the face value. No problem I had them as I was determined not to travel 12,000 miles and not see the game.

The moral to this tale for the Lions organisers is that this is a continual problem facing Lions fans, and you would not have 30,000 supporters going on official tours. Just see it in your heart to fight for tickets for us and we will do the rest. A ballot is fine even a queue then we will have the chance to see a game at cost. I will evidence this problem again later in the book. If the organisers ever read this they will hopefully see the frustrations, don't believe me go on the websites whenever a Lions tour is advertised. See if the organisers have made any progress over a long period.

By the time I had got the tickets I had already made our other plans through a travel company and by making some bookings myself. There had of course been a lot of shuffling but the plan was to see as much of that part of the world as we possibly could as we were travelling so far away. So our plans took in Singapore on the way out, six days in Australia, five in New Zealand and three in Fiji as a recuperation on our way home through Los Angeles. This route chosen in order to circumvent the world ala Drake but a lot quicker and to enable us to completely gain a day by crossing the International Day date line on the way home. The day we would get back would infamously be the 7th of July 2005.

The Lions actually kicked off the tour at the Millennium Stadium, and despite some good performances notably from Jonny Wilkinson and Shane Williams they were outplayed by their Latin opponents, Argentina. Ledesma was outstanding and the Lions luckily snatched a draw right at the death.

Lions fever was by now commencing, there was more coverage in all the media and the feeling that the game was afoot.

Our tickets for the second Test were secured, although still somewhere in New Zealand, I had Stubbies' money transfer document as a proof of purchase, and would pick them up when we met the Sandbach party on the 1st of July in Wellington.

I was by now getting really excited and wondering if the test would rank in my five favourite 'I was there' sporting moments.

1. **Wales 11 v 9 England in the 2005 Grand Slam** – This was only the second Welsh game I had seen, the first being a close loss to the All Blacks in the autumn of 2004. On this occasion no one had given Wales any chance before the game. We had not beaten them since the famous 1999 Grand Slam destroyer at Wembley, and they were the World Champions. It may not have been the best game of rugby ever, but a famous victory was sealed by that Gavin Henson kick and an improbable Grand Slam ensued.

2. **McGinley holing the winning putt at the Belfry 2002** – This was the Ryder Cup cancelled after 9/11 and again, on the final day with Europe level and not the best in singles, no one gave them a hope. When Phillip Price beat Phil Mickleson on the 16th green to win 3 and 2 those of us on the same hole realised almost en bloc that Niclas Fasth would win the cup for Europe if he held on against Paul Azinger. He was going down 18, so hundreds of us ran across seventeen to get near the bunker mound on 18 to see what happened. Well 'Zinger' holed his bunker shot for a half that's what happened and it was left to McGinley playing behind to seize the day with that putt after Furyk had almost holed his bunker shot. I turned to an Irishman who I had never met before to say 'You boys always do it for us' when McGinley holed, there were wild celebrations

which included me and the unknown Irishman jumping all over each other.

3. **McGuigan beating Pedroza in 1985** – My friends Greg Smith, Raf Feliciello and I went to this event with a few others. Raf had been a Welsh amateur boxing champion, Welsh professional Light-Middleweight champion and was then number 8 in the UK at Light-Welterweight. We had a good day in London, the atmosphere was electric and the roof came off when Barry won. You couldn't hear commentary on the night but when I watched later and in the 7th round Harry Carpenter said something like 'McGuigan is falling short with his punches…...oh he got him with the right, he got him with the right, and you can't hear yourself think in this cathedral of noise'………he was right, what a night.

4. **Nadal beating Federer in the Men's Final at Wimbledon in 2008** – As you will read later I have a huge problem with how you get Lions tickets. Well me and younger daughter Laura got these in the Wimbledon ballot and how lucky were we? A great match with the darkness just adding to it, we are privileged to have been there.

5. **Arnold Palmer walking up the 18th at the Old Course in 1995** – If you stand by the right-hand side of the 18th hole you can watch for free. This is where I was when the great man went past, a top moment. I was also there in 2000 when Jack Nicklaus went past but more of that later. Sadly, when watching Seve go

past in 1995 I never thought that this would be the last time I saw him go down 18 live.
THE MATCH WE WERE GOING TO DIDN'T GET IN HERE!

Although the whole experience would be brilliant. I have to say that the Pretoria match in 2009 would get in the top five, again more of that later.

Lisa was then a terrible flyer, and was still concerned about the amount of flying but my late Mom was providing us with some sleeping tablets so we would be okay. Does that mean my Mom was a drug dealer?? Hope not! Most of the flying would have been done by the time we got to Sydney anyway. The Golf clubs as usual would be accompanying us.

The Lions TV adverts were great, All Blacks doing the Haka whilst turning into Maori warriors, faced by British Lions turning into Lions. Even better was the advert which had Lions against All Blacks playing British bulldog, this was commentated on by Martin Johnson and Jonah Lomu. I think Umaga won it, it could have been O'Driscoll, or perhaps Mealamu who joined them and they did a spear dance?? Get it?

It was to be a great summer of sport, the Ashes (the Shane Warne advert was great) and the Open at St Andrews to come. On that point I felt a little let down that Jack Nicklaus was coming back, having made the pilgrimage to see him in 2000 (supposedly his last) which now appears to have been not his last, hence it does not hit the top five. The RBS is now sponsoring him so must have talked him into it, I don't care what anyone says, 2000 was to be his last as it was for the US Open at Pebble Beach. I suppose he can leave whenever he wants, but let down I was.

Telegraph July 2004 –

Jack Nicklaus will play his 33rd Open Championship at St Andrews next year and cannot understand why anyone would not take the opportunity to do the same.

It was thought that Nicklaus had made his last Open appearance over the Old Course in 2000, posing for pictures as he crossed the Swilcan Bridge on the 18th fairway.

It doesn't say that lots of people had made the pilgrimage in 2000 to witness it all!

I had to tape the first game of the Lions tour as I needed to play golf really badly and I mean play it really badly in a medal at the club. I made it through the car park without knowing the score and enjoyed the match. The Lions beating Bay of Plenty 34 v 20, Lewsey had a good game, Shanklin did himself no harm either. Lions won pretty easily in the end although Dallaglio was a loss with his fractured and displaced ankle. Having been one of the few who did not think he should have gone anyway I would not wish to see his tour end this way. Second lost Lion already as O'Kelly had gone home.

Surprisingly Sir Clive did not send for yet another Englishman, I had informed friends that should they present or fax their English birth certificate to Sir Clive they may well get a game. This I have to say was not met with very much agreement, although I enjoyed the moment.

The tickets for the flights and accommodation arrived on the 7th of June. Lisa was by now looking forward to it all. I spent the evening practising my Maori war face whilst Lisa was muttering 'Australia, Australia you bloody beauty'.

I finished off our itinerary, as I do for every trip, then a flurry of e-mails finalised all trips and of course the golf.

Chapter 3

Into the wild blue yonder....... ish

On Sunday the 19th of June I took my youngest daughter, Laura out to buy her a digital camera for her birthday. After that we made our way to my mom's for filling up prior to her dropping us off at the airport. As mom's do there was more than enough food, Lisa did not eat a lot due to the impending flights. My eldest daughter Emma was there and I was chuffed with my Father's Day 'The Alarm' CD, which Emma would tape ready for my return.

Sportswise the Aussies had been beaten three times on the bounce in the one day cricket series... Retief Goosen was leading the US Open. Henson and Shanklin were both looking to feature in the midweek Lions side so looked out of contention for the Test team. We had lost our first game to a fired up Maori side.

The skies were leaden as we got dropped off at the airport. However, undeterred we booked in and sat waiting for our departure whilst taking on alcohol and watching a certain Mr Peterson knocking the Aussies all over the Rose Bowl. As our departure time approached, the airport was hit by the most incredible storm. Planes struggled in and you could see the water trail pouring off the wings. This led to an announcement that our flight would be delayed. No problem as I estimated that it could be for perhaps four hours and we would still make our connection in London; our bags however may not have made that connection. Information in relation to the delay was okay in fairness but it wasn't looking good, our connection plane was still at Heathrow, with a hydraulic problem and there it would remain. I had never had a cancelled flight before and naively thought that it would be all pretty straightforward, it isn't, it's frustrating...very.

Nightmare! Our connection was cancelled and the holiday delayed, this had never happened to us before so we awaited directions. As we did so I saw Gavin Peacock ex Chelsea, QPR and Newcastle, who looked as flustered as we were. I had seen him play once when he was at Newcastle, they were playing Crewe Alexandra, at Crewe. By half time, they were 3 v 0 down but amazingly staged a comeback to win 4 v 3 and that for me seemed to seal their run towards the top flight and something of a re-birth. Gavin scored on that night but he wasn't looking quite as happy this time.

We were directed towards our bags which we recovered and then directed to a very large queue for re-directing us and many others to our destinations.

At this point I rang my local pub the Hawk to confirm that Sandbach were flying direct to Singapore the next morning from Manchester, this lifted my spirits. I was however still hopeful of getting to Heathrow so I asked the BA staff.

'Can I get a hire car?' reply 'you can Sir but our advice is to stay in the queue'.

'What about a taxi?' reply 'I would refer you to my earlier answer '

So in the queue, fagless we remained, however spirits were again raised when a form about compensation came around and I could then while the hours away thinking of how much money they could pay me. In this case nothing as we had not 'been denied boarding' the plane was basically goosed. I would argue the toss over this, bitterly for several months because I believed it was the weather. I lost that battle too. So because of a one hour shuttle cancellation our holiday was to be delayed by thirteen hours and we would lose a night in Singapore. In the queue we remained, and as you do, you bitch about life with other passengers, and of course calculate compensation, for fun, I now realise.

One man near to us was going to Cairns he got a re-route to Sydney, another lady was going to Melbourne she was delayed for twenty-four hours and got the same flight. We got Singapore from Manchester the next day on the same plane as the Sandbach lot and a night in the Radisson Hotel.

Once we had got to the end of the queue I said to the very helpful BA lady;

'Any chance of an upgrade' to which, and to my great excitement she said 'Of course…….' which was tempered by 'we would if it was a BA flight but this is Singapore Airlines sorry'.

Off we went to the Radisson by now tired and having only enough time for me to eat about ten fags and down half that in Guinness. It was too late to eat, so we went to bed.

The next day dawned with a quick breakfast and a bump into Mace and the Sandbach team at check in. I had given them a reference to say that they wouldn't basically trash the VIP lounge and therefore found it quite poignant that I was slumming it downstairs whilst they were VIP upstairs, selfless devotion springs to mind. One of their crew was D who was actually going to New Zealand to see his sister.

D is about 6ft 6" and 18 stone.

I remember the first time I had met him. I used to stand in The Hawk on the TV side at the end of the bar reading a paper, this was before I really got to know anyone. On this Sunday teatime, I stood in the same place and quickly became aware that a sleeping giant was to my right. This giant would occasionally very drunkenly look up and slur at the barman Danny. He was increasingly unsteady on his feet and I thought to myself on several occasions,

'xxxx me if he falls I am going to be crushed against the wall'

To my great delight D then refused his next pint and staggered out of the pub…before returning on the other side, fortunately for me, and demanding his pint.

D is a character, now very much settled down but the source of many a giggle in the pub over the years.

As this example shows;

D to me 'what's that?' throwing down a crumpled piece of paper on the table.

Me 'that D is a Penalty for disorder, how did you get it?'

D 'the coppers locked me mate up'
Me 'what did you do'
D 'told them not to'
Me 'what did they do'
D 'told me to go home'
Me 'what did you do'
D 'stayed for a bit having a go at them'
Me 'how many times did they tell you to stop and go home?'
D 'Loads, then they arrested me'
Me 'That would explain it then mate'

Or…

D 'How many are going on the bus?'
Mace 'With you nine'
D 'That's ten'
Enough said a quality bloke.

By now Michael Campbell had won the US Open and Indianapolis 2005 had been a PR disaster for Formula 1 as a number of drivers refused to race after safety concerns with their Michelin tyres.

Our flight left on time and it was great, the beer just kept rolling in, although by the Himalayas it had run out, much to the disgust of a man behind us who apportioned blame very firmly to 'that bloody Rugby team at the back'. Of course these were our friends from Sandbach. We touched down very early AM in Singapore and bid farewell to the Rugby lads as they made their way towards several Singapore Slings and a connection to Auckland.

Chapter 4
Singapore

We had a good flight but were a bit groggy having flown against the sun, so to speak. There was a bit of a panic over Lisa's golf bag, but it arrived as did our taxi and into the monsoon like rain of Singapore and its muggy heat we went. I of course had to have a fag and found myself in a nicotine infused dizzy euphoria as we got in. It was dawn as we made our way to the Carlton Hotel. On arrival at the hotel the room was of course ready as we had missed one night due to the shuttle delay. The golf that I had requested they had struggled with, but there was an option to play at the nine hole Changi course. This is based around some of the barracks from the second World War the name obviously synonymous with a prisoner of war camp of the same name....

During World War II, following the Fall of Singapore in February 1942, the Japanese military detained about 3,000 civilians in Changi Prison, which was built to house only 600 prisoners. The Japanese used the British Army's Selarang Barracks, near the prison, as a prisoner of war camp, holding some 50,000 Allied — predominantly British and Australian soldiers.

Although POWs were' rarely if ever held in the civilian prison, the name Changi became synonymous in the UK, Australia, and elsewhere with the POW camp.

We decided to get some sleep before deciding on the Golfanygolf. I don't know about you but I always want to have a look around when I get anywhere new, so I spent a good hour up and down in the elevator having a quick fag outside and looking out of our bedroom window.

On the subject of cigarettes, Singapore was my first experience of quite graphic pictures on the packaging of what my insides either did, or could look like. It was really quite horrendous and forced me into covering said offensive pictures with my lighter. It did however make me think, although it would be another two and a half years before I actually kicked the habit.

Anyway, a couple of hours sleep and we were still drowsy, but wanting to grab what we could of Singapore. When I had been in the Navy I had been regaled with tales from the 'old salts' about Singapore and in particular Bugis Street… 'if you have never seen the sunrise on Bugis Street' you have never lived' went the tale. Well I hadn't but I had certainly seen it rise in many other places in the Navy so felt that I was now, some twelve years after leaving the Navy an ex 'old salt'. From our hotel we could walk to the street, which was basically a market place full of the teeming mass of humanity. This eventually led us into Orchard Road, a more modern shopping place. We had a good nose around, preferring Bugis Street and then headed back to the hotel…well the Lions were on TV, beating Southland. A few early doors drinks and then it was a quick change and off for some street food, this time taking the underground which was excellent. The street food market was all a little confusing as there were hordes of vendors all selling food and drinks, and you could, if you wished to, buy from a number of different ones, which caused me the problem. There were tables in the street where you sat to eat, all in all though it was a totally different experience for us and the meat satay, rice and prawns went down a treat.

We then walked to Clarke Quay –

Which was named after Sir Andrew Clarke, Singapore's second Governor and Governor of the Straits Settlements from 1873 to 1875, who played a key role in positioning Singapore as the main port for the Malay states of Perak, Selangor and Sungei Ujong.

We had a couple of very dear drinks, then made our way back to the hotel, as we were by now more than a little tired and we did have most of the next day to further enjoy the delights of Singapore. We slept very well.

The next day dawned and we decided to have a good walk around the area of the hotel before changing to have a Singapore Sling in Raffles writers bar.

As we walked around we were fortunate to see what appeared to be a rehearsal for the National Day, this included some dramatic fly pasts by jet fighters and helicopters.

Singapore celebrated its first National Day in 1966, one year after its Independence from Malaysia on 9 August 1965.

It is a remarkably clean city, probably because of the potential for on the spot fines. However, my view is that if you set a standard and adhere to it then everyone benefits, no matter what that standard may be.

During one part of our walk we could see part of the jungle behind Singapore, which of course many felt was impenetrable at the start of the war. So much so that the defences pointed out to sea.

Unfortunately, the Japanese Army did not think that it was impenetrable, and it wasn't until someone said;

'who are all those blokes on bikes coming out of the jungle?'……

that everyone realised it could be done, by then of course it was all a little too late.

Around mid-afternoon we changed to go to Raffles, having made the effort because we had enquired about it. I have to say I smiled as many denim and beach shorted travellers were turned back at the door. There is no snobbery in this, you can get a shirt and a pair of trousers from shops now for a lot less than a tenner; its standards, simple as that. They make the standard, you adhere to it, you get what you want, or you go to the Long Bar.

Mr NgiamTong Boon invented the cocktail for the colonial ladies.

Enjoy!

Singapore Sling Ingredients
- *30 ml Gin*
- *15 ml Cherry brandy*
- *120 ml pineapple juice*
- *15 ml lime juice*
- *7.5 ml Cointreau*
- *7.5 ml Dom Benedictine*
- *10 ml Grenadine*
- *Dash of Angostura Bitters*
- *Garnish with a slice of pineapple and cherry*

It is the equivalent of consuming a half bottle of wine, so be cautious.

The hotel was named after the 'founder' of Singapore Sir Stamford Raffles, although as per all of our colonial 'discoverers' I suspect that there were probably indigenous people in the area when he got there!

The writers bar is dedicated to the many writers who have stayed at the hotel and written about it. You could also go in the Long Bar where you can apparently throw monkey nuts at each other! Why you would want to do that I don't know. I presume for that reason, the dress code is more relaxed.

The whole place is just full of colonial elegance, it is a fantastic building, full of history, and if you are able you should try it. We had only had one sling each, but that was enough, they were strong enough for us anyway, I was very impressed with how I managed to savour the drink, rather than drink it too quickly as I usually do. Everything about the whole experience we loved. Then it was back to the hotel to change and pack for our night flight to Darwin.

What I forgot to say was that there were red Lions shirts all over Singapore, as there had been in Manchester and on the plane over, the exodus was continuing. Sir Clive had said that he could sense that something very special was going to happen in New Zealand.

Once packed we went into the bar for a few drinks, making sure we put our 'Kuoni' stickers on our left shoulder so that our transport could find us, which he did before whisking us off to the airport. My memory of the airport was of a very spacious place full of light and an outside smoking balcony. The flight was on time and onto our first Qantas jet we stepped.

There were not that many passengers, as it was a night flight I nudged Lisa to get the three seater that was empty to our left, possession being nine tenths of the law in Blighty anyway and we were still technically on Empire soil.

At this point I have to digress to a flight we once had from St Lucia.

Basically we were on the tarmac waiting to go, I was at the window, Lisa to my left, the seat to her left had been vacated and it was apparent that it would be empty. Seeing an expansion opportunity I said

'Mate sit in that seat before someone else gets it'

Lisa, 'I will when we get in the air'

Me, 'No do it now to make sure'

Lisa 'No'

In fairness Lisa like me is a nervous flyer, however the next thing…

'do you mind if I sit here so I can stretch my legs in the aisle?' was the comment from the lady in the centre seat behind us.

'No' Lisa smiled, 'of course not' and the rest is history.

Anyway, back to Singapore…

'Mate sit in that seat we can stretch out'

Lisa, 'I will when we get in the air'

Me, 'No do it now to make sure'

Lisa 'No'

Suffice to say that by the time the move could be made an Australian lady had seized the opportunity and was snoring before we got to the end of the runway.

The flight to Darwin took five hours ish and I watched *Be Cool* on the way starring John Travolta. I loved it he really was super cool in it and seems to get better with age. As an aside between *Grease* coming out, which I think was about 1978 and 1982 when I left HMS Euryalus I had seen the film twenty-seven times, including from behind the screen as it was shown to the officers in the ships wardroom one night. I had even done several scenes with Ian St Paul and I playing several characters as we ran, drunk from visiting the Acropolis, one winters afternoon. I don't know why we were running, we hadn't done anything, perhaps because the hill is so steep.

We had however enjoyed Singapore and vowed to return to Raffles one day.

Chapter 5

Australia, you bloody beauty

There is one thing that I remember about landing in Darwin it was the announcement by one of the cabin crew, that went like this.

'For those of you who are visiting, welcome to Australia'

'For those of you who are Australian, welcome home'

I don't know why but I thought it was a great announcement, I had certainly never heard it before, or since, and it really had a nice ring to it. We had to get off the plane before we flew to Cairns, so a wait ensued for about an hour and once again there was no chance to have a fag, which meant by Cairns I would be desperate. So we sat in a rather sterile waiting room, before boarding our plane again. It was now about 4.30am and we were knackered, but looking forward to the warm weather of Cairns.

The flight was relatively short and did allow us to see a spectacular sunrise over the Gulf of Carpentaria. We were probably too far north to see the mouth of the Flinders River, where Burke and Wills had got to on their trans-Australian walk of discovery in the 19th century. This was of course before they turned for home and the tragic end to their epic journey.

Our honesty on the immigration card got us the full hit once we had landed, with our Golf clubs and shoes subject to a thorough disinfection before we were allowed to proceed, although we had not suffered foot and mouth in the UK since 2001. Hats off to the Australians you can't be too careful, although I was pretty sure the same wouldn't happen to us when we returned to Blighty…and it didn't.

Once through that we got our bus easily and then headed off to our hotel in Cairns. We stayed in the Rydges Plaza, and although it was still early in the morning we got straight into our room. Toby from Kuoni popped by to see if we were okay and explained the somewhat inclement weather for the time of year. Not his problem in fairness.

We had about an hours sleep until we had a pre-booked trip to the Great Barrier Reef. The plan being that we would go across to Green Island, have a look around, do the glass bottom boat thing, then have a sleep on the beach for a few hours in order to catch up on the night flights. Good plan so we went off to No.1 Quay at Marlin Pier and hopped onto our vessel for the crossing. The problem was, despite my insistence on wearing beach shorts, it was proper freezing cold, or at least bad June Blighty weather. The crossing over to Green Island was pretty bouncy as well because the water was choppy as anything. It looked like our sleep plan was not going to work. As we got off the vessel, I was relieved that we were given towels to dry ourselves off should we wish to swim. Not a chance they immediately formed part of our clothing, a very welcome extra layer.

Green Island had been owned by the Craig family since 1971, prior to that for about a million years it was probably owned by an Aborigine family. Maybe I am being facetious as it was the Brits who introduced the west to Australia and as such played a big part in almost wiping out the indigenous population, and stealing their country from them. Apparently old Mr Clarke was a crocodile hunter, and used Green Island to bring some of these noble beasts together. I have to say that 'Cassius' was a magnificent specimen, 100 years old and 18ft long. I do have to say that perhaps the wild was the best place for him, but I had paid to come and see Green Island, so perhaps I should have no say in that argument. We also saw a number of turtles and I wondered how far away the great Eastern Australian Current, as featured in 'Finding Nemo', was. Not far really as it does exist and we were off the Eastern Coast of Australia. Brilliant……

In the 2003 animated Pixar / Disney film Finding Nemo, the EAC is portrayed as a super highway that fish and sea turtles use to travel down the east coast of East Australia. The characters Marlin and Dory join a group of sea turtles, including Crush and his son Squirt in using the EAC to help them travel to Sydney Harbour so they can rescue Marlin's son, Nemo. The basic premise of this storyline is correct. This adds story depth, and gives a general idea of where the exact setting is for Finding Nemo. Every summer, thousands of fish are swept from the Great Barrier Reef to Sydney Harbor and further south.

I kept fish myself, but I have to say that the aquariums here knocked mine into a very large cocked hat. The turtles though had a real soothing grace about them, very elegant creatures, very calming to watch them.

We then moved onto our adventure on the glass bottomed boat, we enjoyed this and especially the knowledge of our captain, and the views of the fish were plentiful and impressive, another good experience. Fatigue was by now kicking in, and the chance of a sleep on a sun drenched tropical beach, had been replaced by a cool wind and clouds, so we went to queue for the return trip to the mainland. We were cold and the wait seemed like ages, we couldn't get onto the vessel and no one told us why……...until we finally boarded and the captain apologised for the delay.

'which has been caused by a humpback jumping in the channel, so the vessel in front stopped to watch'

Great I thought, why didn't we put to sea, so that we could witness one of nature's spectaculars for ourselves. It was not to be, and our trip, despite eyes roving everywhere for whales as we crossed, passed off rather uneventfully.

On arrival at the hotel the Lions test team had not yet been announced, but we did hear that gallant Tim Henman was still in the Wimbledon championships, not for long though he lost in the second round. Despite the fatigue, I managed to drag Lisa off into town for a few drinks and a visit to the Red Ochre restaurant. I had read about it and was particularly interested in the 'bush tucker' on offer.

The service was not very good as they had patently forgotten that we had ordered, however a free drink and the food soon put this to the back of our minds. Lisa had sweet potato and coconut soup to start, whilst I had a mix of crocodile won tons, emu pate (which needed toast not tortillas) and kangaroo, which to me tasted like Aberdeen Angus chicken. Lisa went with the salmon, before falling asleep face first on her plate…ish. We were tired so walked back to the hotel where Lisa went to bed and I had a couple more drinks at the bar. As always there were plenty of Lions supporters dotted around the town.

At 6am the next morning we arose to play golf at the excellently named Half Moon Bay Golf Club, Yorkey's Knob. The course was a bit scruffy to start but then got into several good holes. On the first nine you were not allowed to smoke because of the fire risk. I also found a sign at the back of one of the tees on the back nine, which basically said;

'if you go into the water at the back of the bushes there is every chance that you will be killed by a crocodile'.

I took a very quick picture, then legged it to the safety of the yellow tee. I am not sure that there is even the slightest possibility of death other than by natural causes on UK courses so this was very different. However, in Florida once, on the Osprey Ridge course I saw an alligator basking in the sunshine just off the 7th tee. I asked my playing partners if that was normal to which they replied;

'not in Wisconsin where we come from'

We returned to the hotel, changed, then took a drive up to a place called Kwanda, which was up in the hills, where Lisa would get a chance at hugging a koala. There were also wallabies and other crocodiles. What is it that Koala's actually do? Apart from of course looking cute, feeling cuddly and smelling of eucalyptus. The windy road up and down was a 'bugger' as described by our Kuoni rep Toby but it did allow us some stunning views across Cairns and towards the Great Barrier Reef. We drove into Cairns to have a look at a professional golf tournament the 'Cairns Classic' which apparently featured Mike Harwood who had won tournaments in

Europe and done very well in our 1991 Open, won by his compatriot Ian Baker-Finch. The highlight of the afternoon was at the petrol station where on receiving the correct money from me, the Aussie shop assistant exclaimed 'beauty', it felt so Aussie.

At night we again walked into Cairns and went into Gilligans which appeared to me to be the biggest back packing place anywhere. It was enormous with rooms, live music, happy hour and food all available in a very cosmopolitan environment. We had a look around Cairns for somewhere to eat but did not really see anything we fancied so went back to the hotel for a few bar nibbles and chips. It was another early start in the morning,
4am in fact. Up we got and after a slight scare with regard to the bus arriving we went off to the airport and onto the tarmac to walk to our plane. There were two planes, one a jet, the other propellers, I thought to myself 'there is no way Lisa will get on the propeller plane'. Luckily it was the very small jet, a Bae 146. Lisa wasn't too happy with this one, but on it we got for the three and a half hour flight to Uluru. We had dressed accordingly for the desert in shorts and flip flops but when we arrived it was still early morning and it was freezing. We landed at Connellan Airport, so called after a man called Eddie Connellan who landed his plane at the base of Uluru in 1938. I suppose he then claimed it for Australia (and the Empire!) without telling the indigenous Aborigines to who it is still a sacred place.

So into the freezing desert we went on our coach to be deposited at the Lost Camel hotel. The hotel gets its name from the tale of a Padraic McKee, who set off into the desert on the 18th September 1801 with three camels, having traded the last of his money for them. He was never seen again, and the tale goes that one of the camels can be seen roaming around the Uluru area to this day. The hotel was bedecked in the Aboriginal colours of yellow, black and ochre which I thought was a great idea. The hotel is one of several that are situated around a viewing mound from which you can see Uluru and the Kaja Tjuta range. There is a large communal bar and barbeque area on the far side of the site from the Lost Camel. We even managed to have a little sunbathe as it warmed up, although some non-Brits looked at us a little strangely, they were wearing fleeces after all where we had shorts on.

We decided to respect the Aboriginal wishes with regard to Uluru so watched the sunset from the central viewing point, it was nothing short of spectacular, the colours are fantastic and it was well worth the time spent in getting there for a one night visit. Oh and as was usual on this trip there were Lions shirts in evidence around the camp. At night we walked across to the main bar area for drinks and also took advantage of a huge do it yourself barbeque, basically you pick your meat, pay for it, cook it then eat it, a great idea. I did notice an open letter at the bar, which was from the elders of the local Aboriginal tribe. In effect, it stated that they had been alright until the white man arrived and brought his 'grog' and it asked that everyone refrained from buying drink for the locals. I found it a rather sad indictment of exploration, made a little worse by seeing the locals themselves in the bar worse for wear. This day was also the day of the first Lions test, it was not being shown live so we would have to wait until 5am the next morning to watch it, I didn't look at the TV for that very reason. As we walked back to the hotel there was very little light, which made it quite an adventure, it also allowed us to view the most spectacular night sky we have ever seen. It was almost as if you could touch the milky way, stunning.

The next morning I got up early to watch the Test, it was disappointing, starting off with the 'spear' on O'Driscoll, we never really got going, the line out was a shambles and the Jones/Wilkinson partnership did not work. Sir Clive had said that he sensed that something 'special' was going to happen, well it had to now and we would be at the pivotal Test in Wellington. Because I was up so early I did get a great view of the Southern Cross, in the still very dark sky.

At this stage, Lisa and I had been together for eleven years, marriage had been discussed but we hadn't made the next step. In 2000 I had intended to propose whilst we were in Scotland, one night we were sat in a pub overlooking the Kyle of Lochalsh in Skye. I could see that the sky was spectacular, and thought 'now is the time' so tried on several occasions to entice Lisa out from the pub to the end of a nearby jetty. Unaware of my intention, she wouldn't move so I didn't ask. When I told her what I wanted to do sometime later, she told me that every time I left the pub, people at the bar were eying up our seats, she did not want to lose them so wouldn't come outside! In 2002 I decided that the time would be right when we were at Pebble Beach in California. Basically a piper walks the length of the 1st hole at The Links at Spanish Bay to end play for the day. On this day the mist was rolling over the course, the pacific waves crashing and there were deer everywhere, it was perfect......until the piper got to our point and missed a note (I have it on video) and put me off. Anyway I had decided that sunrise at Uluru was going to be the time and the place for my next attempt.

So, in semi darkness we took our place on the viewing mound to await the sunrise, again the changing of the light and colours on Uluru was absolutely stunning, as the sun came over the horizon I went to one knee and asked the question, Lisa said yes, it was perfect and I think enjoyed by onlookers. Lisa did say to me later that she thought I was tying my shoelace, and I knew I would get hammered at home for not having a ring. I had known Lisa long enough to know that she would have what she wanted in mind and that we could get it at home. In celebration we went to the local café, well it was still very early, then prepared for our flight to Sydney at lunchtime.

Our flight to Sydney was fine apart from a bit of an alarming dip just as we were landing. The directions and information for our shuttle to the hotel was appalling but we eventually got there and jumped in with our fellow travellers. On reaching the hotel the reception was trying to get us to upgrade for a 'harbour view' for Aus$25 extra a night. I am glad we knocked that back as the harbour was Darling harbour not Sydney harbour and we had a bit of a view anyway. The hotel was very big and quite well placed although the concierge did say that Sunday nights meant most places were closed. We ventured out anyway and found the Pyrmont Bridge Hotel which was a nice little boozer and served food. I wasn't hungry but my new fiancée was, so I drank whilst Lisa ate. There were no other pubs open so we got back to the hotel at 9.30pm, I had done a lot of liaison with the concierge desk by e-mail as is my way so with a few drinks inside me;

'is the tour booked?'
'Golf sorted can we get a taxi arranged please?'
'where is Doyle's?'
'where is the Hero of Waterloo pub?'
'can you check my flight time please?'
'who am I?'

You know that sort of thing, the concierge always has the answer wherever you go they are brilliant.

The Lions selection for the second test had not yet been made and I was one of those hoping that Sir Clive would unleash the Welsh backs and give the 25,000 something to shout about. Or would he stick to the 'up your jumper' forward dominance that had won him a world cup? Only time and a couple of days would tell.

At the bar that night I had my fill of bar nibbles, we used to have them a lot in the UK but don't anymore; is that because someone found nine samples of urine in one bowl? Hardly a reason to ban it really? I am more than happy to take my chances although I do note that in a good hotel you always get a fresh bowl, presumably so you can put your own urine in it.

The next morning, we were up early for a road trip around the Sydney highlights. One of the first things we learnt was that the animals on the Australian flag, the kangaroo and the emu were picked because they can only move forwards, good idea. We crossed the Harbour bridge and had our first sight of the Opera House, which is actually beige ish in colour not white as I, or you (if you haven't been) thought. We also sampled the delights of some of the more affluent areas including Balgowan Heights, Seaforth and Manley. We learnt why a certain plant was called 'banksia' because it was named after Joseph Banks who was on the Cook expedition. All in all, an enjoyable morning, after which we were given a sticker with a ship on it and pointed towards an office from where we could catch our trip around the harbour. Unfortunately for us it was the wrong sticker and wrong office, in fact we only had time to berate an extremely rude Korean, who pushed to the front of the queue. My

Korean must have been okay because after I spoke to him he moved to the back of the queue and we got the information we needed. We then walked down to the 'Rocks' had some lunch, found Doyle's and joined our mini cruise ship.

The cruise offered spectacular views of the harbour, as you would expect and pointed out that the Circle Quay boundary of 1788 was a lot further away from the water than it is now, due to building on the original site. After this we had time to have a bit of a rest back at the hotel before a walk down to the 'Rocks' that evening. I was a bit disappointed that a pint of pale ale was A$13 in the Lord Nelson Hotel so despite its being the oldest in Sydney we moved to the Hero of Waterloo where we met a nice bloke from Dublin who had just landed a job there. Apparently, his mate had asked 'does anyone fancy a year in Sydney', he did and here he was. We then moved to the circa 1844 Orient Hotel before Doyle's.

This probably gave us our best view of the harbour as we ate, Sydney Harbour Bridge to our left the Opera House to our right, spectacular. The barimundi and dory went down well and the waiter regaled us with tales of the 2001 Lions supporters and how much he was looking forward to the 2013 tour. All in all, an excellent evening followed by Wimbledon 'live' at 10.10pm! and bed.

The next morning saw a very early start for Moore Park Golf Course a municipal with views of the city and the Sydney Cricket Ground. We had a nice round accompanied on every hole by parakeets. I was amazed at how good the greens were and how much backspin you could get even with a Pinnacle, seriously a Pinnacle was coming back ten feet! Must have been the grass.

The afternoon was spent with a bit of a shopping trip for opals which were gained, but subsequently not really enjoyed. I think we were probably ripped off, although the shop did look okay to us.

We also visited the National Maritime museum, one of the displays told the story of the Batavia;

In 1629, the Batavia was sailing from Cape Town towards the Dutch East Indies, two men Jacobsz and Cornelisz conceived a plan to take the ship, which would allow them to start a new life somewhere, using the huge supply of trade gold and silver then on board. They deliberately steered the ship off course. They wanted to mutiny but basically never got around to it.

On 4 June 1629 the ship struck a reef near Beacon Island off the Western Australian coast. Of the 322 aboard, most of the passengers and crew managed to get ashore. A group including Jacobsz and the Captain Francisco Pelsaert went in search of drinking water. They were unsuccessful so abandoned a return to the others and headed for the city of Batavia, now known as Jakarta. This journey, which ranks as one of the greatest feats of navigation in open boats, took 33 days and, extraordinarily, all aboard survived.

Batavia's Governor General, Jan Coen, immediately gave Pelsaert command of the Sardam to rescue the other survivors, as well as to attempt to salvage riches from the Batavia's wreck. He arrived at the islands two months after leaving Batavia, only to discover that a bloody mutiny had taken place amongst the survivors, reducing their numbers by at least a hundred.

Jeronimus Cornelisz, who had been left in charge of the survivors, was well aware that if that party ever reached the port of Batavia, Pelsaert would report the impending mutiny, and his position in the planned mutiny might become apparent. Therefore, he made plans to hijack any rescue ship that might return and use the vessel to seek another safe haven. Cornelisz even made far-fetched plans to start a new kingdom, using the gold and silver from the wrecked Batavia. However, to carry out this plan, he first needed to eliminate possible opponents.

Cornelisz's first deliberate act was to have all weapons and food supplies commandeered and placed under his control. He then moved a group of soldiers, to nearby West Wallabi Island, under the false pretence of searching for water. They were told to light signal fires when they found water and they would then be rescued. Convinced that they would be unsuccessful, he then left them there to die.

Cornelisz then had complete control. The remaining survivors would face two months of unrelenting butchery and savagery.

With a dedicated band of murderous young men, Cornelisz began to systematically kill anyone he believed would be a problem to his reign of terror, or a burden on their limited resources. The mutineers became intoxicated with killing, and no one could stop them. They needed only the smallest of excuses to drown, bash, strangle or stab to death any of their victims, including women and children.

Cornelisz never committed any of the murders himself, although he tried and failed to strangle a baby. Instead, he used his powers of persuasion to coerce others into doing it for him, firstly under the pretence that the victim had committed a crime such as theft. Eventually, the mutineers began to kill for pleasure, or simply because they were bored. He planned to reduce the island's population to around 45 so that their supplies would last as long as possible. Between them, his followers murdered at least 110 men, women, and children.

Although Cornelisz had left the soldiers to die they had in fact found good sources of water and food on their islands. Initially, they did not know of the barbarity taking place on the other islands and still sent pre-arranged smoke signals announcing their finds. However, they soon learned of the massacres from survivors fleeing Cornelisz' island. The soldiers put together makeshift weapons from materials washed up from the wreck. They also set a watch so that they were ready for the mutineers, and built a small fort out of limestone and coral blocks.

Cornelisz seized on the news of water on the other island as his own supply was dwindling and the continued survival of the soldiers threatened his own success. He went with his men to try and defeat the soldiers marooned on West Wallabi Island. However, the trained soldiers were by now much better fed than the mutineers and easily defeated them in several battles, eventually taking Cornelisz hostage. The mutineers who escaped regrouped under a man named Wouter Loos and tried again, this time employing muskets to besiege Hayes' fort and almost defeated the soldiers.

They however prevailed again just as Pelsaert arrived. A race to the rescue ship ensued between Cornelisz's men and the soldiers. Wiebbe Hayes reached the ship first and was able to present his side of the story to Pelsaert. After a short battle, the combined force captured all of the mutineers.

Pelsaert decided to conduct a trial on the islands, because the Saardam on the return voyage to Batavia would have been overcrowded with survivors and prisoners. After a brief trial, the worst offenders were taken to Seals' Island and executed. Cornelisz and several of the major mutineers had both hands chopped off before being hanged. Wouter Loos and a cabin boy, considered only minor offenders, were marooned on mainland Australia, never to be heard of again. Reports of unusually light-skinned Aborigines in the area by later British settlers have been suggested as evidence that the two men might have been adopted into a local Aboriginal clan. However, numerous other European shipwreck survivors, such as those from the wreck of the Zuytdorp in the same region in 1712, may also have had such contact with indigenous inhabitants.

The remaining mutineers were taken to Batavia for trial. Five were hanged, while several others were flogged. Cornelisz's second in command, Jacop Pietersz, was broken on the wheel, the most severe punishment available at the time. Captain Jacobsz, despite being tortured, did not confess to his part in planning the mutiny and escaped execution due to lack of evidence. What finally became of him is unknown. It is suspected that he died in prison in Batavia.

A board of inquiry decided that Pelsaert had exercised a lack of authority and was therefore partly responsible for what had happened. His financial assets were seized and he died a broken man within a year. On the other hand, the common soldier Wiebbe Hayes was hailed a hero. The VOC promoted him to sergeant, and later to lieutenant, which increased his salary fivefold.

Of the original 341 people on board Batavia, only 68 made it to the port of Batavia.

During this same museum visit I also learnt that in 1616 the Dutch had come across the shores of Australia and apparently reported back to their government or Royal Court that it was not worth any further effort! We nipped in rather sharply some 100+ years later and in fairness have reaped the benefits.

After the museum we had a quick drink in the Dundee Arms then went back to the hotel. In the lift we bumped into Phil Greening the ex-Lions and England hooker and had a brief chat with him. He was a really nice bloke and it all added to the trip for us. That night we were going to go to the Slip Inn where Crown Prince Frederick had apparently met his future wife Mary in 2000. Lisa could not get past the smell of ribs and steak at Tony Roma's so we went in there. Another early start beckoned so we went back soon after to our room. The Lions had put +100 past Mannawatu with Shane again looking good, there had still been no action taken against Umaga for his spear tackle on O'Driscoll and Lions fans were by now wearing 'Umaga wanted' tee shirts.

The next morning saw us on an early taxi ride to the airport with a very entertaining driver. He informed those in our group who were going to Brisbane that the 'Queenslanders were okay but a bit backward' A prime example of this was their calling a lager XXXX because they couldn't spell. He also told us that he had promised to get some of our number to the airport by 6.15am, as it was now only 5.50am 'did they want him to stop or carry on'. Very entertaining for that time of the morning and the airport was reached in plenty of time, we whizzed through check in. Australia had been great but we had so little time, 2013 would see a longer stay.

Chapter 6
What we came here for

We had a great flight to Christchurch the views over the Southern Alps were stunning. An ex UK cop met us and welcomed us at immigration then it was off to our Best Western hotel, which was more like a self-catering flat really, but very spacious. It was here that we realised for the first time that central heating was not a 'norm' in New Zealand, very expensive to run electric heaters were available everywhere. We had a walk into town and visited Chloe's Bar and the Vic and Whale, I liked the look of Christchurch, it seemed big enough without being unfriendly and there were still plenty of Lions fans about. We decided to eat in as we had all the facilities and found that the steak prices were very reasonable. For once we did not have any early start although we hoped for good weather as we intended to go whale watching at Kaikoura the next day.

We were off by 9am and loved the drive up to Kaikoura with the Southern Alps to our left, the weather, although chilly, was gorgeous. If you ever go to Kaikoura from the south don't forget to stop at the look-out point just out of town. The views of the sea and alps behind are really something else. We could also clearly see what was becoming a 2005 tour phenomenon...camper vans. There were loads of them in the car parks of the town, obviously heading to Wellington like we were. We had a huge disappointment down at the whale watching office all trips being cancelled for the day because the water was too rough, it was a sickener but nothing we could do about it. So we set off for Picton on another great run along the coast with seals a plenty. If you have golf clubs you always have an option and I knew that there was a nine holer at Picton, so that was the plan.

As you often see in Scotland the golf course had an honesty box and was NZ$30 for as many holes as we could get in. Set in a valley it was lovely but bitterly cold once the sun set behind the nearby mountain range. We had again picked a Best Western motel and again had the facilities of a flat, we decided to head into Picton to familiarise ourselves with the ferry port. The sight that greeted us I can only describe as breath-taking, there were literally hundreds of camper vans bedecked in Lions and home nation colours. There were thousands of fans milling around, playing touch rugby and generally enjoying themselves. It was only at this time that I realised we were actually part of a sporting crusade, seriously it was an unbelievable feeling, here we were nearly 12,000 miles from home and there were thousands of us everywhere you looked, fantastic. It felt like being part of a very friendly invading army who were being welcomed everywhere. We sorted out the dry run then had fish and chips back at the motel. We did bump into our motel manager who made me mark Haslington and Rhyl on his UK map, perhaps for other visitors. He had lived in the UK and planned to go back at some stage, he had liked the Lake District and hated the M25 so was pretty much on the same level as the rest of us. He could talk the hind leg of a llama (there was a field full of them next door) but was a nice enough bloke and let us have a big heater. We needed it, it was bloody freezing, we even had the oven on so high it melted the paint by the back door. As there was not much light outside the sky was once again, awesome.

A 3.45am start saw us heading for the Ferry Port and the rest of the Lions army. The ferry was at 5.30am, as I had a cigarette outside a couple of Lions fans sent a local taxi off to find a nearby shop to get them some cigarettes. I offered them some of mine but they had a small supply and were obviously very trusting of the taxi driver.

The Cook Straits lie between the North and South Islands of New Zealand it can be notoriously rough so a bouncy crossing to Wellington was anticipated. It was still dark when we set sail, as a result we probably missed a number of sights but the sky was again spectacular with Sagittarius, Scorpius, Crux, Aquila and the Southern Cross clearly visible.

The crossing was fine, flat calm. There was one very green faced Welshman who did not enjoy it one bit. I know the feeling having been seasick in my early Navy days, it is awful. Prior to this I had been sick on a school trip to the Isle of Man so was somewhat of an expert. I got over it in the Navy but will never forget my first trip across the Bay of Biscay. It was rough, I was terribly ill all day, yet still had to clean up for 'rounds' in the evening. 'Rounds' is carried out each night at sea in the Royal Navy and is heightened when it is 'Captains rounds'. The general evening rounds were usually done by the 'Jimmy' the second in command of the ship. When it was your turn to report rounds you had to clean up the 'heads' (toilets) so called because they were usually at the front of the ship where the figureHEAD used to be and the showers as well as the mess deck. By the time rounds started the ship was all over the place. I just managed to survive before another spell in the 'heads', after which I was straight in my 'pit' and couldn't believe that my mess mates were drinking, eating and smoking, whilst I thought I was dying…I survived.

On this voyage, we watched the sunrise over Wellington and docked successfully. As soon as we got off we grabbed our hire car then went off for a rendezvous with Mace at the Sandbach Rugby club base, the Marksman Hotel. They had been on the road for about ten days and had seen the first test, a number of them including Mace and Stubby were of course veterans of Australia 2001. Stubby regaled us with tales of four hundred foot bungie jumps, planes going down fjords, white water rafting, glaciers and paintballing, they had been having a great time. Mace and Brian

Forbes joined us and we set off for our digs in Plimmerton. We stayed with a lovely lady called Barbara at 15 Taupo Crescent; it was like staying with your Nan, home comforts galore.

We quickly dropped everything off then went off to Judgeford for a round of golf. Lovely course, and some stunning scenery. We all enjoyed it though the standard in fairness wasn't particularly good! We then returned to Wellington and dropped Brian and Mace off before returning to Barbara's although it was empty. She had said to help ourselves, but you don't do you? We had been really fortunate in the build-up that the internet was in existence, there was no accommodation available in Wellington for months before. I had somehow stumbled upon a lady who did bed and breakfast in the Wellington area, she in turn put is in touch with Barbara. Although Plimmerton is a suburb of Wellington, it was not too far away and had a good train service to Wellington, which was to be enhanced for the test match. Due entirely to the internet we had got a result, it would have been impossible without it.

Lisa decided to have a rest while I walked down to the station to check on train times for the evening. It was not a long walk about ten minutes, but no sneaky pubs were to be found, which I have to say was a disappointment. No self- respecting UK railway station is without a pub on its door step, opportunity lost!

As I got back Barbara had just arrived so I helped her with the shopping from the car, and we sat eating homemade muffins, drinking coffee and talking about all sorts. Barbara said that there were then a lot of New Zealand parents who were wary about letting their children play rugby. The reason for this being the size of those children with South Pacific parentage in comparison to European ancestry children. No one ever told Richie McCaw or Carl Hayman! Barbara's sons and grandsons all played football. We talked about Wales, England and golf. Lisa joined us just in time for Barbara to tell us about her five week voyage to England when she was younger. She had gone via the Panama Canal and returned via Suez, she had not experienced sea sickness at all during the ten weeks at sea. However on a family trip to Picton, she had become violently ill on the Cook Strait ferry! Barbara was interested to here that I had once travelled 10,000 miles return from Ascension to the Falklands on a ferry (the MV Keren) which had basically been built to cross the channel. I think we all agreed that flying, although having its dangers, was perhaps the easiest way to travel long distances.

We then changed and got the train to Wellington, which took about twenty-five minutes. We passed the Westpac Stadium en route or 'cake tin' as the locals call it. It was a long walk from the station into town and the first pub we got to was an All Black one. We then moved to the 'best British pub' in Wellington the Courteney Arms and I wondered why it couldn't be the 'best New Zealand pub' in Wellington. Prior to this we had gone to Molly Malones to get something to eat, but had seen an Irish lad saunter past and take our table flag just as we approached. In fairness, the place was rammed.

We asked at the Hogsbreath for a table;

'How long?'

Reply 'One……. two…....three hours?'… 'Don't know'

Molly Malone's again 'an hour? If you get a table we will serve you'

Mace text us to advise of an eatery called 'Home star' but it was by now 8.30pm so we dived into Nando's and had a very welcome chicken and something. Lisa was by now asleep but walking with her eyes open so after a quick couple of Monteiths in Luminars we headed back for the train. I was a little disappointed that the lady next to us could neither do the 'Haka' nor tell whether the anthem words were 'God defend New Zealand' or 'God defend our free land'. It is both as it happens although 'God save the Queen' has equal standing apparently……there goes that Empire thing again. We made the short journey from the station, up the hill then tiptoed to bed so that we didn't disturb Barbara who had left us out some goodies just in case.

At breakfast we met two other guests, Earl who was a fly fisher man and told us about the Bay of Islands and every fish in it, together with Ian who had enjoyed Queenstown. Nice blokes and Barbara was great as usual. It was off then to Pauatahanui Golf Club where we were let in by a lady from Edinburgh, it was about £16 for two rounds and a trolley great value. The course was okay and we were treated to no dress code, lager drinking, mobile phones and five balls, but hey when in Rome. For the price, it was brilliant and the weather was tremendous as, once again, was the scenery. Lisa went in the clubhouse where there were a number of ladies, and I am afraid to say unlike some at our own course, she was welcomed with open arms and a barrage of questions about who she was where she had been and all other points. We headed back to Barbara's and it was a quick change ready for the match.

All Blacks versus the British and Irish Lions, Saturday 2nd July 2005
Westpac Stadium, Wellington

Well this is what we had come for, this is what we had travelled, up to then about 14,000 miles for. I was well excited I honestly believed that the Lions, with a load of Welshmen in the back line could take them on and beat them.

The train was packed as soon as we stepped out of the station it was like world war two. There was a noise like an air raid warning with a bloke shouting 'The Lions are coming; the Lions are coming!'...... 'Unite for victory'. You then entered a tent where you could get all sorts of All Blacks paraphernalia, which we did, the atmosphere was bloody marvellous. We took the long walk into town past hundreds of 'have you got a ticket' notes and dived into Subway to stock up. (Classy you may say, see above for trouble finding a table!). Then it was into the pubs the atmosphere was buzzing. The

Sandbach mob had corporate as part of their tickets. Stubby never goes anywhere without getting corporate how he does it I don't know.

Picture the scene…me, a late friend, Pete Barnett and Mace are heading for a bar in Cardiff prior to the England game in 2007. Pete has got us corporate with a family friend. Amazingly we bump into Stubby who 'wasn't going to bother' until offered corporate the night before……enough said.

Back to me and Lisa slumming it, so it was into the Hope Arms and Ferryman for plenty of Monteith and lapping up the atmosphere. I was telling any Kiwi who would listen that the Welshmen in the back line would tear them apart…. they smiled and disagreed. I had never been so excited in my life, seriously, it was being so far from home with thousands of others and the All Blacks just adding to it. In any Lions touring venue they only get this once every twelve years and we were here to see it. We made our way to the stadium and saw touts offering two tickets for $NZ2, 600 we had paid $NZ1, 000 for our $NZ100 tickets so felt perversely like we had a result.

The atmosphere was electric, the Haka sadly drowned out by the Lions fans. This had also happened in Cardiff in 2004 this time by our own crowd and to be honest it just winds me up. It is part of rugby folklore and those who want to should be allowed to enjoy it. I like the New Zealand anthem but the 'Power of Four' used for the Lions on this tour was a bad idea. Why can't we have a verse from each anthem? It would be brilliant.

What can I say about the start? Gareth Thomas the Welsh, Lions captain goes over and we lead 7 v 0, I was going absolutely mental, Lisa had to calm me down. I am absolutely chuffed to say that for those of you who have the Lions 2005 DVD I can be seen going mental. Right at the end of the DVD it shows this try again, but from behind the posts. If you pause when 'Alfie' is behind the left-hand post as you look you will see me in a grey fleece with black shoulders just about to go nuts. Lisa is to my left with the black bobble hat on. Fame at last, for me anyway!

The Kiwi next to me asked why 'Alfie' pats his head so I told him it was basically from the then Cardiff chairman Sam Haman who was a Shiite Muslim. Shiite Muslims in remembrance of Husayn ibn Ali's martyrdom, will mourn for him during remembrance of the Battle of Kabala, by beating themselves on the chest and head. He seemed to like my explanation. At this stage, it was stunned silence from the All Black fans and a sense of anticipation for the Lions fans. We had to keep it up for eighty minutes…could we?

Back to the rugby, Johnny has a kick for 10 v 0, he never misses, sadly he did this time. A great player and servant to the Lions. After this it all rather went downhill as a certain Daniel Carter decided to play one of his best games for the All Blacks. If you have ever read his book, he agrees. He was phenomenal that night. The All Black jersey has a certain 'thing' about it and when I look back now it feels that as I watched as a black shroud came over the stadium and enveloped the red of the Lions and their supporters. They were relentless, despite the best efforts of our boys we were well and truly stuffed although. We did score another try, Simon Easterby going over, very late on. Our line-out went very well, but they seemed to have the ball all of the time, it was a rout. At the end, I had to congratulate my Kiwi friend and we trudged back to the station, with thousands of others. It was a very disappointing train journey back to Plimmerton. We had a few drinks at a pub called the Sandbar and had a quick McDonalds on the way back to Barbara's. She had left out some little reminders like a New Zealand flag, but more importantly a buttered fruit cake, which with a coffee went down very well. I left some All Blacks memorabilia in exchange and we went off to bed. I was bitterly disappointed.

Chapter 7
Journey up North Island

I woke up in the morning feeling pretty much the same but felt that it was an honour to see the Lions in New Zealand. Mace had sent me a text to see what we were doing on Saturday, but we would be home so couldn't meet up. In fact I consoled myself with the fact that I would have seen the series in three different time zones, Australia, New Zealand and Blighty, not many could say that. The local paper was describing the party in Wellington as their biggest for thirty years, so an impression had in fact been made, if not on the rugby field.

We had our final breakfast with Barbara then it was off on the 400+ mile journey to Auckland. Barbara had suggested that we use the 'Desert Road' so we did. It was not so much desert as a different landscape, real volcanoes and we stopped off on our way to look at the 'Craters of the Moon' which was basically a series of thermal vents very spectacular and very much worth the visit. Tornganiro National Park was another spectacular sight. We managed to get to Lake Taupo for lunch and wished we could have stayed longer, the most notable part of the journey, apart from the scenery was seeing 'welcome Lions' banners literally everywhere, and in some instances, there were children out on the roadsides in towns and villages welcoming the invading friendly army.

In Taupo we stopped at Cobb and Co and had a lovely roast pork dinner, with crackling, roasted kumara, pumpkin and broccoli au gratin, it was gorgeous. So was Taupo but in was onwards and upwards towards Auckland.

We got there just as night was falling and had a struggle finding our hotel, a bloke at the airport helped us and we got there in the end. It was in the district of Mangere, and given the security in the rooms and the dodgy hoodies in shadows when we went for a walk it seemed to be a bit of a dodgy place. So we stayed in the hotel bar and had a few drinks, no dinner, it was shut, so it was crisps and that was our lot.

I was looking forward to Fiji for a rest, Lisa needed it, but we had in no way done New Zealand justice and would have to return at some point in the future. We were knackered after a lightning five days in a great country.

Chapter 8
The Journey home

When I started planning this trip I had the idea of flying around the world. I thought we could start off going West which is the best way for catching up and jet lag. We would however, have lost a day going over the International Day/Date line.

For two hours every day, at UTC (co-ordinated universal time) universal-10:00–11:59, there are actually three different days observed at the same time. At UTC time Thursday 10:15, for example, it is Wednesday 23:15 in Samoa, which is eleven hours behind UTC, and it is Friday 00:15 in Kiritimati (separated from Samoa by the IDL), which is fourteen hours ahead of UTC. For the first hour (UTC 10:00–10:59), this phenomenon affects inhabited territories, whereas during the second hour (UTC 11:00–11:59) it only affects an uninhabited maritime time zone twelve hours behind UTC.

Given what we wanted to do and the Test date this was not possible, so we went East and continued to do so, this in effect would mean we gained a day, this day would be the 7th of July 2005. Its significance could not have been apparent when we booked the holiday. After all of our excursions I looked for beach holidays on the way home. In the way were the islands of Fiji, so we booked to stay there for three days.

After unlocking our fortress room at the hotel in Mangere we made for the airport and dropped off the car. We were then subject to that annoyance of having to pay to leave the country. In Saint Lucia once I had enjoyed myself so much I almost refused to pay, although I am sure the accommodation would not have been as good as I had enjoyed if I had not paid. We picked up a few presents in the airport, and spotted some Lion fans mooching around, they may have been the advanced party for the final test.

Our flight was on time and we set off into the grey, cloudy and very turbulent yonder. The first hour was horrendous we were bouncing around all over the place, we never seemed to get above the clouds at all. In fairness, the last hour saw the clouds open up and it got better. The islands of Fiji were soon sighted and the sun was out, this was now our seventh of ten flights so hopefully that was the bad one out of the way.

The one thing I do not like is when the cabin staff are seated, other than taking off or landing of course. This happened to us en route to Chicago once, they stayed seated for the last hour or so at the direction of the Captain as we went through a storm. I was scared to death with sweat running down my forehead, Lisa was in a world of her own.

When we landed the Captain said;

'I am just as pleased that we have landed as you are!' enough said about that one.

Once through customs we were welcomed by a Fijian band it was lovely and got us in the mood. Although this was changed a little when a backpacker seemed intent on holding the bus up forever. She made no apologies for the half hour of my life she had just wasted when she got onto the bus. I have to say I don't care how long anyone takes about anything as long as they don't impose that time loss on my life. If you want to take five hours for a game of Golf...fine, let me through. If you want to faff about talking at a supermarket queue...fine, get out of our way. Etc. etc. etc. you know what I mean.

Our bus driver, Kasim was very informative as he drove along giving us some of the history of Fiji and its language.

Austronesian peoples are believed to have settled in the Fijian islands some 3,500 years ago, with Melanesians following around a thousand years later. According to oral tradition, the indigenous Fijians of today are descendants of the chief Lutunasobasoba and those who arrived with him on the Kaunitoni canoe. Landing at what is now Vuda, the settlers moved inland to the Nakauvadra mountains. Though this oral tradition has not been independently substantiated, the Fijian government officially promotes it, and many tribes today claim to be descended from the children of Lutunasobasoba. Until the 19th century, Fiji's population consisted almost entirely of indigenous Fijians, who were of mixed Polynesian and Melanesian descent and generally spoke languages of the Malayo-Polynesian language family. After the islands came under British colonial rule, a number of contract workers were brought from present-day Pakistan and India, thus giving the reason for the spreading of Urdu and Hindi languages. Fiji received its independence in 1970, but English remained the only official language of the islands, despite being the first language of only a very small minority. After the 1997 constitution, Hindustani and Fijian were given co-official status, although neither are compulsory subjects in schools. There is considerable debate as to whether Fijian should be made the 'national language', to help develop a unified cultural focus, although English and Hindustani would retain official status. Fiji has three official languages under the 1997 constitution; English, Fijian and Hindustani. Fijian is a spoken either as a first or second language by indigenous Fijians who make up around 54% of the population. Fijians of Indian descent make up a further 37%, mainly speaking Hindustani (Urdu and Hindi). English, a remnant of British colonial rule over the islands, was the sole official language until 1997 and is widely used in government, business and education as a lingua franca.

A small number of other indigenous East Fijian and West Fijian regional languages are spoken on the islands, standard Fijian belonging to the East Fijian group. Rotuman and Chinese are also spoken by immigrant populations.

We were staying at a resort on Sonaisali Island, a lagoon had to be crossed first. There were great guffaws of laughter from the Fijians as we stumbled and clambered onto the small boat for the crossing complete with two cases, two sets of golf clubs and a vanity case. Smiling we made it safely on and joined in the laughter as it was very comical. Once we got to the other side we were taken to reception to be met by Vilaume. He was an excellent receptionist, it was just that I was tired and wanted to get in the room and didn't really need telling about all the facilities, food and deals that were on offer. In fairness to him though I probably would have moaned if he hadn't have told me and I lost out, so he couldn't win. A huge Fijian, took us to our room, which for me was the best of the tour. A very spacious wooden hut with a balcony looking out over the sea, it was lovely as were the indigenous lizards on the roof. We sorted out the luggage and wondered why we needed a safe key, when we were on a private island, then went off for drinks and dinner. The food was nice and the Fijian war dance, the Cibi, great although probably better without the music, as we witnessed at Cardiff in November 2010.

Tiredness set in so we retired to the lizards and balcony of our room for a couple of quiet ones and a relatively early night.

We were up early the next morning to play golf, we made sure that we were on the main island for 7.15am, but the bus was late and we were treated to another journey to Nadi airport. This made us late for our tee time at Denerau, but it was okay in the end as we managed to get off at 8.20am. There was a couple in front of us who were a little bit slow, however they did let us through so no arguments there. The course was one of those that are described as 'resort' courses. I think what that basically means is that there are loads of tee options (I was playing off the back which was over 7,000 yards) and you can smash your driver as hard as possible because there is very little trouble to get in, and there is always lots of water. Lisa, as she had done for the whole trip was hitting the ball really well but not being rewarded on the scoring front. I was more than happy with a 77. It was a nice morning to be golfing relatively hot, the scenery was great and the green-keepers knocked a couple of coconuts off the trees for our little treat. Once we arrived back into the clubhouse we were treated like kings or queens and our clubs and shoes handed back in far better condition than we had, handed them to the clubhouse staff.

We were back at the island for around 1pm and had a quick bite before spending the afternoon on the beach. Of note was our trip back to the island when I discussed a famous Fijian with our boat guide;

'Where in Fiji did Vijay Singh live?'
'He is not a Fijian' came the reply, end of conversation. Although I am led to believe that there is still quite some animosity between the 'native' population and the very large Indian population which I am sure led to that comment.

Regrettably there were no catamarans to be had on the beach so I would have to wait until the next day. The afternoon was very relaxing and we caught up on some sleep. The Lions would be playing their last Wednesday game against Auckland in the evening and it had the chance of being a late one. The Lions won the game 17 v 14, there were a number of other Lions fans now on the island having been to either the first or second test or both. All agreed that our countrymen were probably wishing that they were in Fiji instead of approaching a series blackwash against the best team in the world, well it was in fairness a non-world cup year, so they must have been the best, they always are! Whilst watching the match we met a really nice bloke from Auckland who was there with his family, he had third test tickets. He confirmed that Mangere was indeed a little dodgy. He also felt that Joe Rokococo had found fame too early and had lost his touch as a result. He said that his children loved rugby, soccer and cricket and that they cried all night when the All Blacks lost, they couldn't have cried that often. He confirmed that the whole country was crying in 1971. He was in the currency exchange business and thought this easy compared to my job, I would have to disagree as anyone who works for themselves will always have my greatest admiration. Quite wobbly on two legs we made our way back to the room for a couple more drinks that we didn't really need.

I woke up with a mega hangover on what was our last non-travelling day, so I went back to bed but still made it for breakfast which was nice, and made even nicer with the news that London had beaten Paris in the race for the 2012 Olympics, result! We then went for a short walk around the island, as it was overcast and had been raining, practice for home in fairness. The walk was curtailed by Lisa's fear of dogs, she is not very good with them, and as many other people do, gets jumpy. This dog was a very old golden Labrador, must have been at least a hundred in human years and couldn't even have licked her to death. However, the sky was now a little clearer so we went to the beach. I was still bad so had another sleep before having a quick drink to make myself feel better. What actually happens is that you very quickly revert to drunk so don't feel better just a little euphoric instead.

I now felt well enough to set sail on a catamaran. So I went to the man who looked after them;

'low tide' he said much to my disappointment, so I returned at 2pm…

'low tide there won't be anything out until 6pm', more disappointment, so I went for a walk and saw what I think were kookaburras and also some nice green and red birds, there was a sign saying;

'DON'T PICK THE PINEAPPLES' under pain of death, I couldn't see them so I didn't.

After a while I got back to the beach to see that the Cats were out, it was now about 3pm, yes 3pm not 6pm.

So I went back to the man who had said that there would be no Cats at all to-day due to a low tide;

'can I have a Cat please?' I asked.
'they are all booked up', he replied…I was really not now very happy at all, see above;
'I have been up and down here all day and was told that they were not going out!'
'booked up'
'no you do not understand what I am saying, I want a CAT, I have wanted one all day!'
'come back at four'.

So I did and slid off into the Pacific in a slight breeze.

I was once in the Royal Navy but have never really been a sailor as such, I had found on previous holidays that Hobi Cats are ridiculously easy to sail and brilliant fun, hence my insistence. My only other sailing experience had stemmed from a Dartmoor walk that I had gone on in my early days in the Navy. Lieutenant Commander Claro, liked to take the younger sailors out for rambles. I had turned up at one still pissed from the night before. He was not too impressed by my being sick out of the back of the Land Rover so I was ordered to report to him on my next 'make and mend'. A 'make and mend' is basically an afternoon off for sailors, taken from the days when they were given time to 'make and mend' their uniforms. So, on this particular day I reported as directed and was rewarded by the two and a half ringed (Lieutenant Commander) Mr Claro taking me out into Plymouth Sound in his dinghy, it was absolutely brilliant, especially the bit when the dinghy goes over onto one side or the other, and when we passed close to an incoming ship which dwarfed us, I think it was the Bulwark but can't be sure if I am honest.

Why I have never done more of it I will never know, but the feeling of moving along on the water is so peaceful and, when you go quicker, quite exhilarating. Back in Fiji, I poodled around just off the shore for long enough to upset the Cat man so he couldn't go home early. Once I had had my fill I then came back in serenely, sort of. The fact of the matter is that once you get off/out of these types of vessel it is very difficult for me at least to show any style or grace at all. The harder you try the more you look like a bag of rubbish! No points for style whatsoever.

On passing through reception we discovered that our night flight the next day would be delayed by two hours. Not a problem we had arranged to stay in the room until late afternoon anyway. I enquired about another game of golf to be told that the options were Denerau, Denerau or Denerau so we left it. There was a happy hour down at the bar so we gave that a go followed by the curry night which we were looking forward to given the long standing association between Fiji and the sub-continent.

The drinks were great I have to say that the curry night was not, they were all very bland really and tasted the same. The vindaloo was only a medium. I am told that outside of India the curries are watered down anyway as our soft pallets would not be able to take the spice. After this small disappointment, we went back to our room to sort out the cases, then it was back to the bar to watch the State of Origin Rugby League game.

This is big in Australia and is basically New South Wales versus Queensland. There was certainly a buzz around the hotel about it and a lot of sky blue or maroon shirts knocking about. We were entertained pre-game by frog race in front of the TV lounge, first out of the circle won. Most of them hopped it back to their keepers they were not hurt at all it was just a bit of harmless fun in the sand for the punters delight. The match was preceded by

Advance Australia Fair which was excellent and as memory serves me was won quite easily by New South Wales, which gave them the series. So it was back to our room and our adopted family of Gecko's.

The sun shone for our final day on the island so we had breakfast then headed straight for the beach. I had a wander around by the poolside and got talking to a dairy farmer from the West coast of New Zealand. We discussed our trip, he agreed that we had not spent enough time in NZ and that the next time a tour of both West Coasts on both islands would be a good idea. He said that he had been on a similar type of trip. He and his wife had gone to Sydney then driven to Perth. From there they had gone to the UK to work before moving on to Scandinavia, Russia and Berlin before the wall came down. I agreed with him about the greyness of East Berlin when the wall was up. I had been there myself in 1985, the other thing we did agree on was the value for money of New Zealand meat compared to the UK. I then returned to the beach before a quick run back to our room which we had booked until 6pm.

I slid the key in several times but it wouldn't work so I went off to reception.

'my key doesn't work'
'sorry you can't have the room until 6pm there are people waiting for it'

'sorry? You agreed that I could have the room until 6pm we have planned our day around it, no one has told me otherwise'

'sorry for the inconvenience you may have it until 3pm' said the Duty Manager.

'and you want me to pay for it as well?'

'Yes F$50'

'why should I pay when I am the only one who has not been told what is going on? It should be complimentary'

'okay' said the Duty Manager.

Lisa was not at all pleased but it was better than nothing. We still had a couple of hours left on the beach which I spent trying to count the islands that I could see, there were too many, apparently about three hundred in all. We cleared out of the room bang on 3pm and alighted to the bar where we were assured we could shower a bit later on, as our flight was not until midnight. So we enjoyed our last happy hour had a bite to eat and then said our farewells with a last journey across the lagoon.

Our plane was an Air Pacific jumbo and looked colourful sat on the tarmac. I was by now looking like a beetroot due to the late burst of sun, so thought I would try my hand at check-in;

'any chance of an upgrade?' I asked.
'yes, no problem F$1200' came the reply.

I decided against it, though did think we had a result by getting a F$40 voucher for food due to the delay......it never happens in Europe!

Lisa had a veggie burger and fries, her second fries of the day! I went for the burger and fries, ten Benson and Hedges and three Fiji beer option. Well you have to, don't you?

On the subject of upgrades, I have heard many stories of people getting them, however having flown many thousands of miles I can honestly say that we have not even come close to getting one. It may be that I have a habit of wearing the same scabby old pair of grey shorts I have had since purchased in BHS Amiens, France in 2001 and usually some sort of Lions tee shirt or top! (I am adding this paragraph in December 2012 and still wear them!) (Finally blew out in 2015)

Our flight over the Pacific was uneventful, except we crossed the day date line. This meant we had set off from Fiji at midnight on the 7th and arrived in Los Angeles at 4pm on the 7th, pretty good as a quirky thing, the date though was awful.

In Los Angeles we saw the odd straggling Lion fan, it really is quite amazing where they, (we?) pop up. I had a chance of a quick fag then it was off to the gate for another overnight flight, this time to London on British Airways. Although we were both now absolutely knackered sleep did not come to us easily. It didn't help with the ladies in front of us reclining to the full extent of the seat. The flight again was not really eventful.

Unbeknown to us a tragedy had been unfolding in London on this fateful day. We landed at Heathrow in the early morning of the 8th to the sight of the front pages reporting on the bombings, it made me feel ill it was an awful way to come home. We were lucky, we got home safe and sound.

We had to take a plane from Heathrow to Manchester, this flight was entertaining to say the least. The pilot was a proper comedian even commenting as we went over Slough with regard to the address of the 'Office' which at that time was a hit on our screens, starring Ricky Gervais. We landed safely and got home with no problems. The only problem we now faced was that which faces us all, the tidying up after being away, all the washing, all the ironing and work looming after the week-end. We got on with it gave our presents to loved ones and moved back into normal domestic life. The cats, Sammy and Harry were pleased at our arrival after showing their usual initial displeasure that we had left at all.

One thing was for certain, it was South Africa next and we would be going.

Chapter 9
The Wait

There was talk over the intervening months of the Lions bubble having burst so comprehensive was the defeat, although the mid-week team under McGeechan had been undefeated. This nonsense however was put to bed and the Lions moved on.

I had a few things to do before 2009. The wedding was one of them and convincing Lisa that South Africa was safe was the other. I have to say everyone who has been says how great it is, others write of the doom that awaits the non-wary traveller. My view was, as always, that bad things can happen anywhere in the world and if you take advice you should be okay.

It was apparent from Stubby and Mace that their trip would be a slimmed down version of what they had done in New Zealand, and would feature only themselves and another legend Matthew Alton.

On the 7th of October 2006, a little earlier than we had planned, but helped greatly by our respective mothers, Lisa and I were married at Crewe Hall. It was a sparkling October day and could not have gone any better if we had written it. I started the day by playing in the medal at the Golf club and then meeting my brother and his partner at the Hall before getting ready as Wales got badly beaten once again in a World Cup qualifier. One of my last remaining ambitions is to see the Welsh football team in the final stages of a major tournament. We were agonisingly close in 1978, 1986 and 1994 where Joe Jordan, Scotland infused by the death of the late great Jock Stein and a Paul Boden penalty miss respectively thwarted us. The fact remains we have not qualified in my lifetime and at the time of writing this section of the book I am fifty years old.

In 2016 Wales qualified for Euro 2016 in France. I kept my promise and was there for the first game against Slovakia in Bordeaux. A great experience that I had waited my entire life to see.

Back to the wedding, Lisa had been given a very eventful drive in a Bentley en route to the hall by our friend Brian Preece and all went to plan. We had a quiet but elegant wedding breakfast with close family, Carol an old work friend of mine and Greg a very old friend from Rhyl with his now wife Jen, the only non family. At night, we had a hundred and twenty guests, including the Half Wits and friends from work and had a hoot right up until 3.30am in the morning when Lisa and I finally went to bed. It was a great day and substantial hangovers abounded the next day. Very very enjoyable.

In 2007 there was a World Cup to be enjoyed, I had thought and looked at being in Marseille for two quarter finals which would INEVITABLY have involved Wales. I am glad I didn't book as Wales struggled throughout the tournament and were knocked out at the group stage after a brilliant game against Fiji, so much for plans.

I am not sure when it was, but Lisa finally agreed to go to South Africa, and by the end of 2007 I was making our plans. Once again we would aim for the crucial second test and see as much of the country as we could before and after this date. The company with whom we booked, Deva Travel of Chester were brilliant, as with all these things, itineraries constantly change…or mine do anyway. The only odd thing was that we would fly through Dubai on Emirates both going out and coming home. I presume this was part of the Emirates deal for flying to South Africa, hoping that people may stop off. We decided to do just that.

Our final itinerary would be to fly to Dubai from Manchester, stay over for two nights then fly to Johannesburg. We would stay there for three nights, take in the Pretoria test match, then drive to Isandlwana for two nights. From there we would drive to Durban for a night before flying to Port Elizabeth and driving towards Kenton-on-Sea for a two-day safari. We would then drive to Plettenberg Bay, George, Hermanus ending up with our last two nights in Cape Town.

It sounded like a plan. All it needed now was planning as we would be booking our accommodation in

Dubai and George. Golf of course needed sorting and the all-important tickets for the game.

As all the planning was going on our own little scrum half, Euan was born on July the 15th 2008 to my eldest daughter Emma, so we had a new arrival to send cards and buy presents for when we went to South Africa.

Chapter 10
Here we go again

It was an omen it had to be, in February 2009 we travelled to Edinburgh to watch Wales play Scotland in the six nations opener. As we were walking up a street outside Murrayfield, with no one around, none other than Sir Ian McGeechan came walking towards us. He was brilliant and had a photo taken with me which has pride of place on my Facebook wall. I have to say that without exception every rugby player that I have ever spoken to, asked for an autograph or asked for a photo has done so with no problems whatsoever. They are brilliant in every respect. Will Greenwood who I had taken a dislike to after his 'try' sign against Wales in the 2003 World Cup was one of the best of the lot. I approached him at Twickenham for an autograph for a friend's son, he walked twenty yards to put his drink down then came back across to sign, quality bloke. As was Jamie Roberts who I saw once in Regent Street, he let us have a photo no problem whatsoever.

The best of these moments ever has to be Dan Carter. Lisa absolutely adores him. A friend of ours is the international TMO, Graham Hughes. Graham did us a favour after the 2009 Barbarians/All Blacks game by getting us into the players' lounge. He knew Lisa liked Daniel. As Lisa and I were talking, with her back to the players I heard;

'Gooders!' I looked behind Lisa to see Graham coming towards us with Dan Carter, as he got to where we were I said to Lisa;
'There is someone to meet you mate' indicating behind her. She turned to see Daniel right in front of her and in a fluster thrust out her hand and said;
'Hi, Daniel nice to meet you', he shook her hand and moved on to other fans.
However a short while later I spotted him at the bar and sort of gesticulated for him to come over, he did and we got a great picture of him and Lisa on her phone, having forgot the camera. Quality people all.

Back to the tour, we had decided to stay at the Atlantis in Dubai as we had got a deal, to play at the Emirates and also to visit Fancourt whilst in George, on the Garden route.

As I have mentioned earlier I was now on Facebook so decided to try to use this in order to get tickets for the 2nd Test. I had already looked for opportunities but once again the advice was that you needed to go on an 'official' tour in order to get tickets. This is absolutely ludicrous it was by now well known that thousands of people travel on Lions tours and the majority are NOT on official packages, it is completely a corrupt practice allowing monopolies to form, and more frustratingly allowing the black market to thrive. My Facebook, South African contacts looked promising at one stage, however it was not to be, although I was very grateful for their travel advice. I ended up buying two £40 tickets for £400+ from a ticket site on the internet. My thoughts were that at least I had them and could sell them if I got a better deal.

In the autumn of 2008 the financial bubble burst and businesses very quickly started going belly up. This had a knock- on effect on the corporate packages set up for the Lions tour. In effect some people could now no longer afford to go on them and it became apparent that the Tour may not be as full as everyone thought....... that was wrong. The benefit of the demise of some of these tours and the fact that the South African public thought the prices were exorbitant meant that tickets at legitimate prices came back onto the market.

I discovered this when perusing the South African ticket sites one morning, I saw that tickets were available for Pretoria. Not quite believing my luck I rang the ticket office in South Africa and bought two at cost price......result! However I now had two others that I needed to get rid of. I put them back on the site where I had bought them and managed to sell one. The other did not sell so I decided I would take my chances of selling it in South Africa.

On returning from the tour I pleaded with the Lions company to look after the faithful fans on the 2013 tour to Australia, and more importantly make sure we got the biggest stadiums. They didn't…again!

The last checks I made before we went, as always, was a visit to the Foreign and Commonwealth Office website where there is great advice for travellers. South Africa has a reputation for crime so it is always worth doing. The main point I picked up on was that some visitors were being followed in their hire cars from Johannesburg airport and then car-jacked. As a result I cancelled the idea of picking up a hire car and arranged a lift from the hotel.

It was a good choice, as I perused South African papers before we left I read of three Lions fans being the subject of the very same modus operandi and they had lost everything. I also took in advice about locking car doors, leaving a car length gap between yourself and other vehicles at junctions and traffic lights and taking hotel advice on where you should and should not walk.

I did find some of the internet information disappointing, particularly from South Africans who outlined the horrors awaiting the Lions fans and those who would attend the World Cup a year later. Lions wise there was that car jack and I heard of one other attack on a drunken Lions fan walking in the wrong area at night, bad news for him, but overall not anywhere near as bad as anyone would have thought.

So we were ready, prepared and had the Tour meeting with Mace, Stubby and Matthew lined up for Johannesburg.

Chapter 11
Zig zagging our way to Johannesburg

If you look at a map of the world you will see that the journey from Manchester to Dubai then onto Johannesburg is in fact a bit of a zig zag. We were about to take it on, like thousands of other Lions fans.

The 1st Test in Durban had been and gone, at first the Lions looked out of their depth, once they got to grips with it, they clearly were not and could so easily have won the game. It was great to see the sea of red at the game, but disappointing to see empty seats, not many but empty seats. I will bet my house on the fact that there were ticket-less Lions outside that ground, the empty seats being for the 'organised' tours. Up to the point of the first test the Lions had played some good rugby, most pleasing of all had been the thumping of the Transvaal in the Bok homeland. Nevertheless, the result gave us hope, and as we had done in 2005 we travelled with the series already in the balance.

My Mom, once again took us to the airport, there were no Lions about we whizzed through check-in and went straight to the bar. It was Monday the 22nd of June. The only highlight in the bar was my Eagle of the 12th hole on the Old Course at St Andrews, this was on the Nintendo DS but I could now lay claim to being the only person, or one of the very few who could claim to have eagled the same hole for real and on the DS, having achieved the feat that March on the Old Course for real. Great start.

Slightly tipsy we boarded the plane for our night flight to Dubai, I usually have a plan to while away the hours on planes. This one involved a number of cans and a couple of films. It was our first flight on Emirates and the reports had been good. Unfortunately, this crew had their own plan which went something like, feed them, give them a drink then turn the lights out. So, after a number of requests for drinks went unanswered I settled back and watched the great in- flight entertainment, dozed a bit and awaited the approaching dawn. According to the flight map I saw the sunrise over Iraq and the Tigris, which was good, if it was right, and we landed safely in Dubai at around 6am UAE time.

Terminal 3 at the airport is nothing short of fantastic, glass everywhere, tumbling waterfalls, it is huge and you feel very much that you are in the Middle East with men in freshly pressed thobes in abundance. Everywhere looks and feels cleaner than a very clean thing and you could spend hours just wandering through it all.

Another tip I had picked up from Trip Advisor was to buy some booze at the airport off licence before leaving, so I went and bought four bottles of wine. Good idea the hotel prices were generally very high.

Taxis were in abundance so we jumped in and headed off for the Atlantis. They drive a bit quick in Dubai, don't they? We sailed past the Creek Golf club with its Dhow sails, and witnessed the huge building programme which is going on, and as the recession bit looked like it was about to stop or had done already. We also saw a lot of unfinished buildings, part of the recession we supposed. The Burj Khalifa was hugely impressive and seemed to go on into the sky forever. Our journey took a lot longer than I expected but eventually we turned onto the road that had been built into the sea leading to the Atlantis. We had seen the Burj-al-Arab to our right as we approached, that was impressive but the Atlantis was huge. Set at the end of a palm tree shaped manmade island we could see it from miles away. One noticeable thing about all the other buildings was the number of them and the number that were unfinished. I have to say there are that many I would be surprised if they ever sold them.

The taxi fee was about £4 and considering it had taken about thirty minutes was an absolute bargain. The hotel itself was a wonder, I would describe it as in between garish and stylish, some of the things in it were unbelievable, for example the fish tanks in the 'lost Chambers'. It was very busy but we checked in by

7.15am and had our room to boot. We snatched a couple of hours then had to get ready for a trip to the Burj-al-Arab for afternoon tea.

Again we took a taxi, and were dropped off outside with a brief walk across to the front entrance. It is an imposing building and your neck cranes in order to get a good view. Once inside you can take photographs but no video, as we discovered when we got the camera out. The staff were incredible from entering the door until we left, and the tea was excellent, sitting overlooking the Gulf and the rest of Dubai. There was plenty to eat, you could have as much as you wanted and there was a glass of champagne to boot. It cost around £150 for the two of us but the experience was worth putting it on the plastic. The hotel is rated as seven star, I have to say I don't really get why they had to go over five stars that denotes the quality anyway. If I had to be picky it was certainly impressive but had nothing like the elegance of say, Gleneagles, a five-star establishment.

After a relaxing hour or so we left into the heat of the afternoon for my next research project.

I had read that the markets or souks in Dubai were well worth a visit and that Al Karama may be worth a jaunt so we hopped into another taxi and headed there. We got out into the heat, it was really stifling by now, and found ourselves in quite a large square with a number of shops surrounding it. We started to have a look around but as is almost always the case we were approached by the stall holders with offers a plenty.

After a number of;
'we are just having a look'

we were approached by a youngish Asian bloke who perhaps had sussed that we were not customs or anything else. He asked us the usual questions, we said we were after handbags;

'Do you know Primark?'
'Yes' we said.
'My shop is called Primark come with me'

I have to say that we were intrigued so followed him out of these shops and into a dusty street. He crossed so we followed and found ourselves outside 'Primark' which was in fact a very small shop. Our friend unlocked the door and invited us in encouraging us;

'Look, look'

There were loads of bags but Lisa said that they were not that good, sensing this he opened a door in the back, which was locked and invited us to look further. The bags looked better but still nothing for Lisa. He then unlocked another door and motioned for us to go up the stairs. I have to say half way up I got a little edgy, but everything was okay.

I didn't need to worry; if Aladdin's Cave was real and in the middle east then we had just found it, Lisa's eyes lit up. After a good while browsing we purchased several quality bags at quality prices. Seeing that I was clearly a follower of fashion our friend snatched on the opening of our purse-strings and said;

'Do you like tee shirts?'

I said yes and we were off across the road to his friends' shop, where I bought several LARGE polo shirts for a good price. We left Karama with a spring in our step destined for the Gold and Spice Souk to finish off our shopping.

The shirts were actually not as large as I had hoped for. I discovered this on our return to the hotel and left them all stretched over my case overnight. It didn't work and I eventually sold them on to Mace who fitted into them slightly, or a lot better than I did.

It was by now mid- afternoon and the water was going down at about half a litre a second, and as we had dressed up for the Burj uncomfortable was our middle name. We sloshed on regardless and took the taxi to the Gold Souk where we had a brief look around and I bought some saffron, cinnamon sticks and vanilla from the Spice Souk. We then took a great 10p ride on a dhow across the creek, the sounds as we crossed and the views given that this is in the old part of town really made the day. As did our search for a watering hole when we found Waxy O'Connors. The drinks hit the spot and it was into our fourth taxi of the day for a return to the hotel.

The roads were very busy and the trip highlighted by a near miss as we nearly ran into the back of another vehicle. There was a proper screech of brakes which shook us up a bit. No problems for our driver, he didn't even blink. The sunset made the Burj Khalifa and the Burj – al – Arab look even better and I could swear that the sun was coming down through the Arabian arch which is in the middle of the Atlantis Hotel, as we approached.

The afternoon tea had sorted out any need for dinner, the Lions were on TV and my Golf case was damaged. So we had a relaxing evening watching the game, drinking Rose and me sewing my case up. The Lions drew 13 v 13 with Western Province a tight game played out in a storm in Cape Town. We had of course been up all night so sleep did not take long to arrive.

The next morning was bright and hot and we were up early for a game of golf at the Emirates. Much to my disappointment I had been told that the Majiis was closed due to course work so it was looking like the Faldo. I had a slight problem, as I had almost sawn my left thumb off ten days before we left, and had only had the stitches out two days before.

That tale is worth re-telling;

The neighbours to the rear of us had allowed us into their garden to cut some branches off a large Ash tree which actually stood in my garden. We had left a couple of branches on to take off the following year. They had wanted us to cut the trees down but I had refused, as they were nice and gave us a lot of privacy. One afternoon Lisa had rung me at work to say that she had got home to find the branches cut off and devastation in our garden. The washing line was down, there were bits of tree everywhere and our potatoes had been flattened. I went home and straight round to the neighbours to ask who had cut the tree, the man of the house said they had, I couldn't get angry as he has Parkinson's. However, I was seething and returned home in that mood to commence clearing up. He came out to see and was visibly upset at the mess in our garden. His wife subsequently rang to say that we had gone into their garden without asking to cut off some branches. This was clearly not the case as her husband had helped us with a piece of rope and their son had asked for some of the wood. When told this she then said that the 'tree surgeons' who had done the work had got our permission to go into our garden, they clearly had not and she was told so. She later came around and tearfully offered us a plant as recompense which we grudgingly accepted.

Back to the devastation; the branches had been left behind and if nothing else I thought I would claim them for our wood-burner. So, still in a foul mood I started furiously cutting the wood and clearing up. You will know what happened next, and it did, I missed and the saw went into my left thumb. As you do in these situations the shock hit me before the blood did, there was a lot of it. I went into the house and showed Lisa, she does not do blood but agreed it needed looking at. I decided to try to get the Nurse and the local surgery to assess whether it needed stitching. Once I took off the tea towel it was a resounding yes, so it was off to A&E.

After a bit of a wait and an excruciating 'look' and poke around into the cut, for which I had bravely declined anaesthetic, it was decided that surgery was required due to the fact that I had nicked a tendon.

I was told to await the call to surgery the next day.

I went to work and was called in at 9am, a little earlier than expected. I got to the hospital and awaited my call. At one stage I was in pre- op but got turned around for a more pressing case. My next visit saw me taken in and I remember drifting off under the gas. The next thing I knew was that I was being woken with a concerned consultant and several nurses around my bed.

The operation hadn't gone ahead as I had started to vomit whilst under and it had all gone very dodgy with the consultant being pulled in to sort me out. It was apparently a close thing and I have to say it shook me up when it sank in. The staff however were great and it was decided that I should have a local instead. So I watched the Doctor stitch me back up and gratefully returned home, pleased that the stitches would be out on the day before we left for the holiday. What a way it would have been to go, stupid really but there you are.

So, taxi to the course which was conveniently situated at the end of the Palm. The traffic in Dubai almost constantly seems to be going back on itself with each road having some sort of switch back which is all down to planning I suppose.
The Bedouin tent clubhouse was soon seen and we entered the air-conditioned clubhouse to sort out the paperwork. The lady said that our tee time had been cancelled, I had the confirmation in my hand, she said that we may not be able to play.

I said very politely;
'I have come a long way to play, we have paid our green fee and I am not leaving here until we play'.
I also saw a note which showed that the Majiis was open so added;
'And I would like to play on the Majiis as well if at all possible please'
The lady rang the company who I had booked with and we were soon on our way to the practice ground, as an added result the booking company paid the difference for upgrading to the Dubai Desert Classic course.

We had a brief practice it was very warm; my thumb was a little dodgy so I decided I would tee the ball up to protect it. I loved the course it was a totally different experience. Grass and desert, it was great. Lisa despite a breeze and loads of water had to stop playing after nine and seek the shade of the buggy. I was fine the breeze was perfect for me and I did not find it too bad. I was pleased to get a couple of pars, I almost holed out on the par three 11th and had a par on the 18th. All in all a great experience, well worth the visit. The staff in the clubhouse gladly sorted out the taxi back for us so we returned to the hotel, to discover the good news that my youngest daughter, Laura had gained her degree in Art, and just as importantly, the water park was open for guests.

I love water parks, I don't know if it is being brought up on Rhyl's open air baths with its diving board, or the paddling pool being at the top of our street.

What I do know is I do not like roller coasters but whether it is 'Summit Plummet' at Blizzard Beach, the 'Black Hole' at Butlins, the 'Python' at Waterworld or the 'Kamikaze' at Fuengirola if it involves water and adrenalin then I am up for it. The waterworld at Atlantis did not disappoint. I did manage to get Lisa onto the relaxing creek, which as you know is a relaxing drift around the park on an inflatable, she (who loves roller coasters) was having nothing to do with the rapids or anything else.

So I, along with the other children had to make do with the 'Shark' and the 'Leap of faith' all on my own…again and again they are so much fun, as long as you don't find your bathers disappearing up your backside too inconvenient! Lisa had taken to the sun, or more realistically hiding from it under a shade, and after several hours of rides we returned back up to the room.

After a quick change, we decided to go to the 'Edge' outdoor bar where they were doing two for ones, this meant a pint of Heineken was in reality only £3.50 and not £7 which was a bit of a result. We had booked dinner at the 'Levantine' and had a great meal of kebabs, sparrow and lamb, the dancing entertainment was also very good and we rounded off the night, and our Dubai visit with a couple of Disaronno's at £6.50 each! We even spotted the TV chef James Tanner in the bar. We made the drinks last forever, although another early start beckoned in the morning.

In the morning, the sense of anticipation had returned, the Test series was very much up for grabs now. It was a good job that we left plenty of time for the trip to the airport as the traffic was horrendous. Fortunately our driver knew a short cut and we got there in plenty of time. I did see our first front row of the tour. It probably wasn't meant but there were three blokes leaning up against a wall waiting for something or other and they looked like a front row, with the hooker in the middle, half the size of his companions on either side.

We were, as were most others on the plane left frustrated for an hour once we had boarded, as two passengers failed to get on, so their bags had to be removed. Why would/does anyone put their bags onto a plane then not get on? Apart of course from terrorists, but that I suppose is why you get left feeling frustrated.

Although an hour late the flight, again with Emirates was one of the most enjoyable I have ever had. There were loads of Lions fans on it and the beer was flowing. I spied my favourite tee shirt of the tour, it was basically a man at a bar just about to pick a pint up with the steps up to his drinking it also depicted with the words 'Crouch, touch, pause, engage' written at the various stages. The bloke who had it on did tell me that there was a more risqué version available for later in the tour.

At around 2pm I decided that I was going to have a few, so left my seat and stood next to the galley to drink and watch some of Africa pass by below us, I had a great afternoon. When I got back to my seat, Lisa informed me that the man sitting at the end of our row of three was an Emirates pilot from South Africa and he kindly pointed out several of the areas of Johannesburg as we came into land.

It was light when we landed, but getting dark, so I was glad we had arranged for a pick up from the hotel. We also liked the fact that as we came out into arrivals there was a sign saying 'Mr and Mrs Goodwin' just like on the films, waiting for us. We didn't see much on the way into the hotel, but enough to know I would have got very lost and hence very frustrated and concerned. The hotel was fine a 'Southern Sun' in Sandton, there were 'Gulliver's Travels' clients all over the place. These were the fans on the rather expensive package tours, this made any sale of my odd ticket looking a bit bleak.

We took advice from reception and were told that it was safe to walk to the shopping plaza across the road, the 'Nelson Mandela' centre where we would find bars and restaurants. We did as advised and found hundreds of Lions fans doing exactly the same thing. We had a few drinks and a meal of steak and chicken which was less than £20. South Africa really was cheap as chips in comparison to anywhere else that we had visited. A couple more drinks in the bar and we retired for the night. There were a couple of great series marketing things in the hotel. One was a size chart where you could compare your height to the Lions or Springbok players. The other was a large picture of a number of Springboks with the head cut out of one of them, where you could place yours just like those that you see at the fair. We also discovered that our 'worldwide' travel adaptor was actually 'worldwide apart from South Africa' so we borrowed one from the concierge and confirmed that we would give it back in Cape Town!

The next morning it was Golf at Kempton Park, 'where Ernie learnt to play' or so it said on the website. We got a taxi to the course which was miles away and took a good half an hour. It appeared to be in the middle of dodgyville but I am sure it was all very nice.

Something you have to get used to in South Africa is gangs of men congregating on corners, mostly in the morning. It can appear quite intimidating but I am reliably informed that they are merely waiting on the chance of work. Employers basically pitch up if they need workers for the day, pick them up and off they go. The clubhouse, at the course was quite large and the cost was £14 for both of us including two trollies. As we were on the high veldt the grass was very yellow in colour and a bit reminiscent of those old films of Phil Bennett gliding across the field in the 1974 tour. Initially it was freezing cold, but it warmed up and I did not see, from me anyway, any sign of the ball 'going further at altitude'. The course was fine, there were several really good holes and the greens were excellent. My only problem was the walk from the ninth to the tenth which was about half a mile and towards 'dodgyville'. This part of the course was actually walled in. On one tee, we were waiting for those in front to clear, or at least I thought it was those in front, it became clear that it was two lads meandering through the course. I have to say I got more and more concerned as they kept heading straight for us, right up to the tee. In the UK they would have been told, or asked to 'please move' a long time before this. They walked straight onto the tee, had a look at my Footjoys, which had the Welsh flag on each heel, then went on their way, it was very surreal, and to be honest quite unnerving. We, however finished the round with no problems in bright sunshine and left the course to the corporate group who were warming up as we left.

Our taxi guy was back soon enough and we got back safe and sound to our hotel.

Once back we decided to do a bit of shopping and to collect our tickets, which we could do in the supermarket in the mall across the road. We picked the tickets up after a bit of a wait and also got two bottles of wine for £3.50, the Amarulla was only about £4 so it was bargains all round. It may have cost to get here but it was now cheap for most things. The hotel was a seething mass of Gulliver's fans, and the team had now been announced, there was to be no Shane Williams but Simon Shaw would play, presumably to front up Mr Botha. I have to say by now I was getting very excited as were most of the other fans. I had not sold my 'spare' on the site on the internet so I would have to try to get rid that night or at the ground. Mace, Stubby and Matthew were staying quite a way from us so we had arranged to meet outside the ground.

I had found a restaurant to try before we got to Johannesburg, it had been recommended to us by the hotel and was called Linger Longer. I asked about walking and was told to walk only a hundred yards either side of the hotel or to the mall, so we asked for a taxi and were directed to a rank across the road, 'they are safe' the receptionist said. Village Vision they were called. There was a white gleaming Mercedes there so we thought we had got another result. That driver directed us towards a cab at the back which was a very run down purple Mercedes driven by James. I told him where we wanted to go and he set off and took us to Le Cunard……. twice, I told him where we wanted to go again, and we set off to find it, it was now clear that James did not have a clue. This was one of the hairiest taxi rides of my life as everywhere seemed dark and forbidding, not like any other city centre. James was talking in his own dialect, I now know to get directions but at the time was thinking anything. At one stage, we turned into a dead end and a car appeared behind us…. just appeared! So I locked our doors. I was panicking, sweating, my heart was going at a rate of knots and I was really concerned for our safety. It was ridiculous in hindsight but if you had been there, and read about Johannesburg then you would have been to. It was so scary there were no lights anywhere, there were stray cats all over the place and no one was walking. We didn't see that many cars. At one stage I demanded that we be taken back to the hotel. James kept reassuring us that everything was okay, and it kept looking more dodgy outside of the car. Then, as if it was an oasis in the desert, we saw lights, and the restaurant sign. Even when we got to the car park of the restaurant there was a guard at the gate, but relieved we got out and given our journey entered into another world.

Linger Longer was a very, very classy establishment, five star in every sense of the word, and the price was amazing. I had the crocodile and prawn starter, Lisa, Blue cheese and avocado followed with impala and a chicken dish which with a bottle of wine and a tip was less than £50. It would have been double that at home. James was waiting for us when we got out, and got us safely home and in doing so got a good tip, it had been an experience. I went back into the shopping mall to see if I could get rid of the ticket, there were no takers, so it was back to the Amarulla and Disaronno in the room before an excited night's sleep awaiting the game in the morning.

Chapter 12
Springboks versus the British and Irish Lions, Saturday 27th June 2009

Loftus Versfeld, Pretoria

When I awoke the excitement and butterflies hit me immediately. We decided to go across the road to get some money and also buy a Free State Cheetahs jersey that I quite liked. We then got back to the hotel after the breakfast queue had gone down. There was red everywhere and the 'Gullivers' group even had Gareth Chilcott there to guide them through the day.

He made his England debut against Australia in 1984, and toured with the British and Irish Lions in Australia in 1989.

After breakfast we got changed into our Lions tops, whilst I played some of Winston Churchill's finest on the iPod, it was all very rousing stuff. As we came down into reception I had to have a picture taken with the

Springbok cut-outs, and hoped that their performance would be just as stilted that day.

As I said before the public transport in South Africa at the time was either non- existent or to be avoided so we had arranged for a taxi from the hotel. It may sound strange but this was actually a cheaper option than anything else, and the cost was very reasonable to boot. Our driver was Ali and he was perfect given his wealth of local and historical knowledge.

So off we headed up the N1, which Ali told us was also known as the Cape to Cairo road. Because if we kept driving north that is where we would eventually end up. Unfortunately, we didn't have time. The road was teeming, and I mean teeming with red shirts in a variety of transports it was, again like an army moving northwards. We asked if we could stop off at the Voortrekker Monument and Ali obliged. He also told us about the history of the building and basically why it was there. It was built to honour the settlers who had come up from the Cape a couple of hundred years previously to settle in the Pretoria and Johannesburg areas. I pointed out to Ali, and he confirmed that actually they had not made any discoveries as the indigenous people had been in the area for thousands of years anyway. So they were the first white settlers. I found it quite confusing that Pretoria was the administrative capital of South Africa with Johannesburg, the 'capital'. We had a brief walk around the monument then it was off into Pretoria where Ali took us around Church Square.

Church Square - *is the historic centre of the city of Pretoria, South Africa.*

Its most prominent feature is the statue of the Boer leader and president of the first South African Republic Paul Kruger at its centre. Several historically and architecturally significant buildings surround the square: the Palace of Justice, the Old Capitol Theatre, the Tudor Chambers, the Ou Raadsaal (Old Council Chamber) and the General Post Office .The turreted Palace of Justice was the scene of arguably the most famous political trial in South Africa's history, the Rivonia Trial. During this trial, Nelson Mandela and a number of other prominent liberation struggle figures were charged with treason and subsequently incarcerated.

The most amazing thing I found about the square was that amongst a sea of black people enjoying the sun and picnicking there sat an elderly white couple on a bench completely oblivious to the striking memory they were creating. Why I find it so striking still I don't know, perhaps because we very rarely saw white people without cars until we got towards the Garden Route. Or because in that small-time frame in that one place it showed the country as it is, a black African state.

As we headed up towards the ground the red shirts started becoming more and more dense. Ali dropped us off opposite the ground and I immediately sought to off load that ticket. We were just too late at the doors of one pub as two tickets went for SAR1,850, each, about £150, that would have done me. The bars in this area were a little too busy so we went to the drinks park outside the ground. I found it hard to see a green shirt it was a sea of red, absolutely fantastic. There were Lions supporters dressed as Lions, one as John Travolta, another as a Welsh Chubby Brown, and two mighty mouse with Brian O'Driscoll and Jamie Roberts as their faces. It turned out that of the 45,000 crowd, 30,000 were Lions supporters, that so far from home is and was phenomenal and it was great to be a part of it. We had made contact with Mace, Stubby and Matthew so all we needed to do was sell the ticket.

We went for a quick walk across the road with me in my best 'I am not a tout' voice shouting;
'Anyone need a ticket? One spare'.

A couple of people took my number, however just as I thought trying to sell it by the ground may be a better option, a taxi dropped off what looked like a father and son with some friends. I asked if they all had tickets, they said they needed one and we negotiated SAR1,300 which was about £100. I gave the ticket to the lad with all the supporting documentation to show I had paid twice that and now very pleased with myself we walked off for the meeting with the chaps. In effect I had paid about £520 for four tickets and got £320 back so my tickets had cost me £100 each, which was better than New Zealand after all.

Stubby, as is his gift had managed to get himself, Mace and Matthew into a complimentary drink do. The tickets only got them two drinks, so we waited outside for them with a six pack. We had a couple of great pictures taken with Lisa in the middle of the front row of five as the 'hooker' and enjoyed another hour or so before kick-off shooting the breeze. We even caught a glimpse of Phil Bennett asking for directions near the drinks park. In fairness, the last time Phil had been at Loftus, he had got a bus straight in and put the Springboks to the sword on the 1974 tour. The atmosphere outside the ground was electric.

As we walked up the stairs to our seats Lisa said 'Iain who is that?' pointing to a man near to us, I looked and was amazed to see that it was the great Wales Rugby Union and Great Britain Rugby League star Jonathan Davies. I immediately asked if we could have a picture and he obliged; the day was getting better and better.

The atmosphere inside the ground was fantastic, it was amazing a sea of red wherever you looked interwoven with specs of green, what a sight. The sun was out and Loftus added to the atmosphere with its steep sided stands. We were about ten rows from the back of the stand between the halfway line and try line at the end that the Springboks would attack in the first half.

There may have been better test matches over the years, but this one had it all. Drama, absolute commitment, ferocity, swings in the fortunes of both teams, and a final climactic ending, it was almost visceral. It really was enthralling and I feel privileged to have witnessed it.

The Lions had decided to put Adam Jones in against the beast Mtawirra, the latter having conned the referee into letting him do what he wanted to Phil Vickery the previous week. Luke Fitzgerald had also come in, as had Simon Shaw, a veteran of 1997, who perhaps had his best ever game at test match level, he was awesome. Rob Kearney started in place of the injured Lee Byrne. As is the case with most second tests, it was really the series decider, the Lions either went on to Johannesburg with a chance of winning the series or they went home having been beaten.

The first minute saw the first incident, when Schalk Burger gouged Fitzgerald, at the time I was glad we had only fourteen in opposition for ten minutes, on seeing the highlights furious that he hadn't been sent off. He would be banned as other Springboks would after this game. This gave the Lions the chance to strike first with a penalty, Kearney then went flying in near the corner to our right. Stephen Jones another hero of the game slotted the conversion, as he would all day and it was 10 – 0.

The ferocity was now very evident it was a hard and at times brutal war of attrition, especially up front, where our old friend Mr Botha was putting it about. From a line out the Lions defence was broken and Pieterson scored, Pienaar, as he did on several occasions missed the kick. At this stage despite the collisions it became very cat and mouse before we went in at half time with a 16 – 8 lead thanks to Stephen Jones boot and a reply from Francois Steyn. It was a very hopeful Lions support who broke for the toilets at half time, Loftus was dry of beer, but we had, had enough before the game. There were however loads of cans being passed around by red shirts in the interval.

Jones extended our lead to 19 – 8 with a drop goal, early in the second half, and we were looking really good, however injuries were taking their toll. We lost Adam Jones, Gethin Jenkins, Jamie Roberts and Brian O'Driscoll in the second half and in the end had O'Gara and Tommy Bowe as our centre partnership. O'Driscoll went off after a huge collision with Danie Roussouw in midfield. When you see the replay, it epitomises how the Lions placed their bodies on the line that day, O'Driscoll just threw himself into the collision, which left the mountain Roussouw staggering around, dazed, he too had to go off. Adam Jones had been cleared out by Botha, in fairness, Bakkies didn't deserve the ban he later got.

As we moved into the last quarter we were looking good then Habana struck and after another penalty our lead was cut to one point. Another Jones penalty took it to 22 – 18 and it was fingernail, edge of your seat and butterflies time. It was at this stage that the key moment in the game arrived, the magnificent Jaques Fourie took the ball right on our left touchline and head down headed for the line. O'Gara missed the tackle as Bowe and others closed in, Fourie went to ground the ball and did so……was he in touch? From where I was standing yes he was, from the TV pictures yes he was, could you really give a try? No, did they give a try? Yes and heartbreakingly the Lions were 25 – 22 down.

We had led up to the 74th minute it was gut wrenching, but the drama was not yet over, a limping Jones again nailed a penalty and we were level. This will do I told myself still in the series going into the last match.

I still find it hard to take, writing and thinking about it now, we missed touch with another penalty which could have given us field position for a drop. Aerial ping pong commenced until at about 79 minutes and 55 seconds the ball fell into the arms of Ronan.

He who closed matches out for Ireland and Munster with aplomb, this time, and I can see it now he runs and motions, beckons the Lions forward with his hand, the crowd are practically screaming 'Kick it into touch!!!!'……he launches a Gary Owen……chases his own kick and touches De Preez whilst he is in the air. Penalty! The rest as they say is history the local hero

Morne Steyn, slots the kick from his own half and the Lions are beaten.

The Garryowen is more often than not attributed to the Irish team of the same name who used the tactic a lot less sparingly. Of course, it is also the name of a song used by the 7th cavalry under Custer prior to his last stand. Maybe this was Ronan's?

We and the Lions were forlorn, I have never felt so bad at a sporting event ever. I also had to feel for Mace, Stubby and Matthew this was the seventh consecutive loss by the Lions that they had witnessed. I remember just sitting with my head in my hands as the Springbok crowd rejoiced around us it was terrible, the sun which had been blazing away all day disappeared, as if in mourning.

As we walked from the ground, I felt that even the Springbok fans celebrating around their braai were a little embarrassed by it all, maybe it was wishful thinking, although there was very little banter as they could see how bad we were feeling. Good as gold Ali picked us where he said and we made a very subdued return to Sandton. We stayed out and went to an Indian that we had booked called Bakhara where I was perked up a bit by Ostrich Tandoori. The other supporters had the same look on their faces, the re-run back at the hotel did not make matters any better, so we just went to bed, it was horrible, gut wrenching, you name it we were feeling it. But we did now have the rest of South Africa to look forward to.

Chapter 13

Escape from Johannesburg

I have to say I did not sleep very well that night. It was not the game that was concerning me it was the self-drive out of town in our hire car. I had even gone for the hotel delivery so that we were not singled out by anyone at the downtown office. Ali had given us a pointer on how to get onto the N3, however it looked far too complicated for me. I had sussed out a longer but easier route for us to go which involved heading north on the N1 then branching off onto the N3. It was about ten miles out of our way but meant fewer, traffic light stops and lessening any potential for being car jacked. I have to say my hysteria was caused solely by the news I had read and some daft comments in a local paper by a 'local' which effectively suggested that all foreigners were likely crime subjects in South Africa.

I was basically awake at around 3am and just lay there waiting for the morning and our break for freedom, in hindsight it was all a little daft, but better safe than sorry. I hardly ate breakfast, we got our things together and I was delighted to see that we had been delivered the whitest car in history! It may as well have had a target on it for good measure!

With trepidation, I turned left out of the hotel, so far so good, I then drove two junctions until we came to a set of lights. This was a right turn for Ali, but a straight across for me, regardless whether any other traffic was coming or not and onto the N1, after about ten miles of driving northwards the N3 sign appeared, and the butterflies started receding.

Once onto the N3 I relaxed and told Lisa about my concerns;
'I knew there was something up with you all morning, now I know why.'

For those of you reading this don't be put off, all the people who we met in Johannesburg were brilliant, just follow their advice and you will be absolutely fine.

This was the advice I published on Trip Advisor;

I took Foreign Office website advice and did not hire a car from OR Tambo but got the hotel to pick us up. I also got the hire car dropped off at our hotel when we left Joburg. I felt a little edgy driving out of the city but that was PURELY down to what I had read before and also some outrageous comments on the Star website a few days previously on a blog when some Lions fans had been hijacked. These were South African comments and were unneeded and poor for their country. We spent two weeks in South Africa drove from Jo berg to Durban and then PE to Cape Town we had our moments but it was absolutely fine, just be sensible like you would anywhere. I have driven in many countries and at times felt uncomfortable in Miami and places in the UK. Just do everything you would at home and you will be fine, a great great country to visit. I hope the scaremongers do not put off the World Cup fans.

And the reply I received from a South African contributor;

Hi iantoes

Many thanks for your insight into the reality of driving in South Africa. For a tourist it is no problem. In metro areas just take normal precautions as you say you would in the UK Your point is also well taken about reading South African Internal websites - especially those based in Joburg! The people posting on some of these sites are only equalled in their apparent negative views of everything within their own country by posters on the BBC "Have Your Say" website and readers of the Daily Mail!

Chapter 14
History in full technicolour!

Our trip to Kwazulu Natal took us through a number of familiar sounding towns, Newcastle followed by Dundee. Nqutu was the first town we came across where we saw our first township, and I have to say from the road it all appeared not very nice. In fairness we didn't visit so we don't know, it just seems that almost twenty years after apartheid there are still the have's and have not's. This can be the same in every country but the gap can be a lot wider in some. We saw some ostrich and Stenbok on our way and after several hundred miles approached our destination at Isandlwhana Lodge.

The run up to the Lodge saw us driving over very rough terrain but in the sunshine, it was perfect as was the backdrop of Isandlwhana itself. It does look like the sphinx. There were even ladies washing their clothes in the river, it was all very rustic.

The lodge was fantastic overlooking the entire battlefield, with rock dassie's all over the place.

During my childhood, Rhyl library was like a second home. It was ideally placed on the way home from school across the road from the Police Station. In the junior section above the door was a Zulu shield and assegai, for years it had me transfixed I never got bored with just looking at it and wondering about the people behind it. After watching both 'Zulu' and 'Zulu Dawn' I even found the thought of these people quite frightening but even more intriguing. Now I was in the heart of their Kingdom it was brilliant.

The lodge was really nice, although as night fell it got a little draughty, having said that the fires and small bar took the draft away and we ate a lovely dinner but for calories sake missed out pudding and bread. This did not stop us drinking a load of Heineken in bottles, after Lisa went to bed I stayed up with a few, and as I would watched 'Zulu Dawn' on the TV/Video in the guest lounge. I was even given the keys to the place by the manager and asked to lock the place up!

The sky that night was fantastic, you could almost touch the Milky Way and the moon was like a reverse nimbus it was breath-taking if you like your night sky. I eventually wobbled to bed looking forward to our tour in the morning.

Breakfast the next morning was lovely served by a gorgeous and very shy Zulu lady who we could quite happily have wrapped up and taken home.

Our guide for the day was Rob Gerrard;

ROBERT GERRARD FRGS Rob is the son of Brigadier BJD Gerrard DSO who commanded The Gordon Highlanders, that regiment which Winston Churchill called The finest fighting unit in the British army and the great-grandson of Sir John Robinson, the first Prime Minister of Natal. Rob was educated in Britain, commissioned into the British army, served with The Gordons in Kenya and on secondment in Malaysia, Borneo and Thailand. In 1969 he left the army and moved to South Africa where he became a commodity trader. His passion for British military history led him into lecturing on the battles of the Anglo Zulu War of 1879 and the Anglo Boer Wars of 1881 and 1899-1902. He was made a Fellow of The Royal Geographic Society in 1998. Rob's compelling talks on the battlefields are moving and insightful. He not only talks about the military strategies and tactics, but he weaves stories of the people involved into his presentations, which help his guests experience these battles emotionally and from the historical perspective.

The tour started on the lodge veranda in bitter cold, made a lot better by woollen ponchos, we had the same vantage point as the Zulu leaders Chiefs Ntshingwayo kaMahole and Mavumengwana kaMdlela Ntuli. one hundred and thirty years before. Rob's voice was a great story tellers voice and the whole thing was re-created in front of our eyes. It was fascinating. From afar we were shown the location of Younghusband's last stand, Durnford's Donga, and the Cave where the last soldier is believed to have retreated to before also being killed. Once the battle had been 'set up' by Rob we moved down to tour at the foot of the Isandlwhana to see all these things for ourselves. We then got to sit down in the glorious sunshine to listen to the full details of the battle. The most evocative thing for me was to look to our left on the ridge where the lodge was and imagine being one of the soldiers who looked up to see four thousand Zulu warriors appear on the skyline, who then placed their shields next to them so that they appeared to double in number. Just before they crashed down onto the British Army. It must have been absolutely terrifying. What made it all the worse was that there was a solar eclipse at the height of the battle, I cannot begin to think how bad it looked and then it all went dark if only for seconds!

We paid homage at the Umphafa spirit tree and the Zulu memorial:

Umphafa is said to bring the spirits of the ancestors so that they can be buried. After the battle, family members of killed Zulus would've taken branches of imiphafa (that's the plural of umphafa) and waved them around over the battlefield to capture the spirit of their deceased relative, then they would've taken the branch home and used it in the burial ceremony to lay their soul to rest.

We then returned to the Lodge for lunch. In the afternoon, we made the short journey to Rorke's Drift, situated under the Oskarberg hill, so named after a Swedish King. The 'drift' was named after James Rorke who settled on it as it was the only crossing point over the 'Buffalo' River, he apparently shot himself. We were seated for a lot of the tour at the very spot where Henry Hook VC received his medal. Unlike the film, he was not the person portrayed by James Booth but an extremely brave man rightly rewarded. The actual buildings are a lot different to what we saw on the film. The hospital for example was quite detached from the redoubt. One of my favourite bits of the film is the roll call the morning after the first attacks;

Colour Sergeant Bourne 'Hitch? Hitch? I know you're here laddie I have seen you, you are alive!'
Hitch – 'Oh am I Sergeant thank you very much'

Or words to that effect.

Private Hitch VC with Corporal Allen VC made an incredible fifteen journeys across from the redoubt to save men in the hospital when, in the words of our guide Rob 'everyone in the Zulu nation was trying to kill them!'. At one stage Private Walters at night used a black shawl to get across the same space in order to disguise himself from the impi. How any of these men survived is beyond me, but survive they did. Perhaps some of it was down to 'Pip' the dog who patrolled the ramparts and barked as the night attacks came in.

Colour Sergeant Bourne DCM lived until he was ninety-one, he was twenty-four at the time of the battle, and became a Lieutenant Colonel. In 1936 he gave an interview for the BBC 'I was there' sadly it has been lost.

The medals awarded were as follows;

Awarded the Victoria Cross

- *Lieutenant John Rouse Merriott Chard, 5th Field Coy, Royal Engineers*
- *Lieutenant Gonville Bromhead; B Coy, 2nd/24th Foot*
- *Corporal William Wilson Allen; B Coy, 2nd/24th Foot*
- *Private Frederick Hitch; B Coy, 2nd/24th Foot*
- *Private Alfred Henry Hook; B Coy, 2nd/24th Foot*
- *Private Robert Jones; B Coy, 2nd/24th Foot*
- *Private William Jones; B Coy, 2nd/24th Foot*
- *Private John Williams; B Coy, 2nd/24th Foot*
- *Surgeon James Henry Reynolds; Army Medical Department*
- *Acting Assistant Commissary James Langley Dalton; Commissariat and Transport Department*
- *Corporal Christian Ferdinand Schiess; 2nd/3rd Natal Native Contingent*

In 1879 there was no provision for the posthumous granting of the Victoria Cross, and so it could not be awarded to anyone who had died in performing an act of bravery. In light of this, an unofficial 'twelfth VC' may be added to those listed: Private Joseph Williams, B Coy, 2nd/24th Foot, who was killed during the fight in the hospital and for whom it was mentioned in dispatches that "had he lived he would have been recommended for the Victoria Cross".

Awarded the Distinguished Conduct Medal:

- *Gunner John Cantwell; N Batt, 5th Brig Royal Horse Artillery (demoted from bombardier wheeler the day before the battle)*
- *Private John William Roy; 1st/24th Foot*
- *Colour Sergeant Frank Edward Bourne; B Coy, 2nd/24th Foot*
- *Second Corporal Francis Attwood; Army Service Corps*

On 15 January 1880, a submission for a DCM was also made for Private Michael McMahon (Army Hospital Corps). The submission was cancelled on 29 January 1880 for absence without leave and theft.

After his army service Frederick Hitch became a cabbie in London and was buried in Chiswick, to this day cabbies still attend his grave. The whole day was an experience and a half, if you get the chance you should go.

Dinner was a little spoilt by some gents from some rugby club or other (I actually know which one but won't embarrass them here) who loudly regaled most of the room with tales of how someone they knew, rather than themselves, had been extremely intimate with some lucky lady or other usually in Hong Kong or Thailand, what the ages of the ladies were I know not. It was Isandlwhana Lodge 29th June 2009, boorish given that there were couples and families present, shame on you, whoever you are.

We had experienced a lovely stay so it was very much time for bed, although we had ensured that our conversation was kept to ourselves rather than the whole dining room.

We awoke to another lovely sunny day, had breakfast then set off through the Zulu lands over many, many really potholed roads, some alarmingly deep, towards Durban. We travelled through a number of towns, including Melmouth and Eshowe. One noticeable thing about the very dramatic landscape was that there were clearly a number of 'table mountains' in South Africa. We saw several on our trip through the area and I am presuming that the flatness was caused by a glacier going across the top of the mountain, only a guess but I am going to stick with it. If anyone else out there knows the real reason then please let me know.

The whole trip was without any real incident apart from a stop for drinks and Biltong en route. I did get a little lost around the Umhlanga (pronounced Shlanga) Rocks area, but we eventually found the hotel without any problem, another Southern Sun, the Elangeni. It was still sunny so we went for a stroll down the promenade, which was quite busy and bought a couple of craft presents for our respective mothers. We had a couple of drinks in the perfectly acceptable hotel bar then had dinner in an Italian restaurant at the hotel next door.

There were a number of teams staying at our hotel who were playing in the beach soccer world cup. I had a couple of pics taken with the Nigeria and Morocco teams and it was back upstairs to pack for the early ish flight in the morning. One of the hotel managers had been really helpful by finding a tube for us to put my Mom's African painting in and overall, we thought the hotel was just fine for an overnight stop.

We got up the next day had a quick breakfast and after getting a quick update on the route to the airport set off. I am dreadful at getting directions, I always want them in a hurry, never fully listen and surprise, surprise end up in the wrong place on many occasions. This was one of them it was a 'left then left' out of the hotel, which we did, however I didn't do the 'go across the first road then turn left' bit. So we ended up down by the docks in the early hours with no one around other than dockworkers who could not speak English just like we could not speak their language. After a lot of huffing and puffing by me we eventually found a sign for the airport and followed it onto the motorway. As soon as we got on it was backed up for miles due to a crash. Time was now becoming of the essence as we had a fair chance of missing our flight to Port Elizabeth. Luckily for us the traffic jam moved quite quickly past the crash and we got to the airport in time, dropped the car off and booked in. The lady at the desk was extremely helpful ensuring that we were not charged for the clubs by using our full allowance for all bags. In February this year (**2011**) British Airways at Heathrow were not so obliging charging us £80 for 'excess baggage' when the truth was that we were still under our personal allowance overall.

I digress, at the airport the choice of South African Airways planes was fine but they all looked very small. Lisa was not happy, but fortunately as we had at Cairns in 2005, we walked past the propeller plane and onto the jet. The journey to Port Elizabeth was great and we whizzed out and into our last hire car of the trip. We had to come back on ourselves for the next destination which was the Kariega game lodge near to Kenton-on- Sea. So we travelled back eastwards through Port Elizabeth and onto the lodge.

Chapter 15
Safari and the Garden Route

It was out of season but very much to our benefit as we were given a fantastic four-bedroom wooden lodge overlooking a drop into the game reserve and beyond. It really was quite an amazing sight overlooking the canopy and wondering what all the noises were. Our walk down to lunch was also interesting as there were a number of very large footprints around and about which certainly were not human. The food was fantastic and the choice amazing, if you have ever been on a cruise, you will know what I mean. There are a number of 'meals' available but somehow in a buffet setting you end up having bits of a number of meals. The dining room was very busy and our friends from Gulliver's travels were all over the place.

We had an hour or so to relax before we were picked up for the afternoon 'drive', our companions being two Irish couples and Terry and Susie from Wales. They were all very pleasant, as was our keeper Wynand. There were two sides to the park, referred to by one of the Irish ladies as 'Disney' and 'Jurassic Park'. The difference being that we were never going to be killed by anything in 'Disney' apart, perhaps from a charging rhinoceros or two. We saw rhino, giraffe, lions, waterbuck, eland, baboons, zebra, wildebeest and monkeys. At sundown we stopped for a 'sundowner' which rounded off the day perfectly. As is the tradition in these things we ate our evening meal with our group and Wynand who with the Irish contingent went off into the night to seek some other animals. We stopped with Terry and Susie to round off the day with a few drinks then it was back to the Lodge as an early start beckoned in the morning.

A sumptuous breakfast gave us a great start to the day and our first sight was of warthogs, we saw most of the animals that we had the day before, but the highlight after much searching was a bull elephant, it was magnificent. As was the bit when Lisa said to me 'I haven't got a picture of a giraffe yet' to be immediately confronted by a giraffe that was close enough to touch.

Another very large lunch was followed by my cycling up to reception to see if they could change us some money. It was all uphill and against the wind, I was knackered by the time I got there, coming back was better, although the wildebeest did not enjoy being disturbed twice. We had time for a quick drive into Kenton to get some money and a bottle of Rose to go with another one of Amarula all for £11, what value.

The 'drive' that afternoon saw our Irish friends replaced by a family of Swedes from Gothenburg along with Terry and Susie. We went on the river for a couple of hours fishing, without catching anything then found a hippo and her calf near to a river. It was by this time dark and the experience was enhanced because it was so dark. We once again had dinner as a group, and found the Swedish family to be really nice and very helpful. It was at this dinner that I found out that the 'clicking' language I loved so much hearing was 'Xhosa'. They also told us that whales had been sighted at the Tsitsikamma National Park so I made a note to stop off as we drove along the garden route. We again had a couple of drinks with Terry and Susie, who were going home the next day, and went off to our very large lodge. It had been another great day, we did have the choice of going on another drive the next day but decided to make an early ish start for the drive to Plettenberg Bay. We tipped Wynand as is the tradition and hoped that it was enough, about £20 in sterling. I have to say that I thought if every couple did the same he would have made a few quid over the season, he had been a good host.

The next morning, forgetting that the morning 'drives' start very early we went for breakfast at 815am, it had finished, however a little Xhosa lady got us some bits together and we were fine. As we drove away we saw Terry and Susie walking down for breakfast and told them to run! We said our good byes and it was off on the road again.

After Port Elizabeth I suppose we were on the garden route, the scenery was certainly stunning enough anyway. There were no whales at Jeffery's Bay or at the Tsitsikamma National Park but the mountain range was great, as was the bloke in the garage who gave us directions.

We stopped for money at Jeffrey's Bay and I spent a very nervous twenty minutes outside the bank waiting for Lisa, incorrectly thinking as it turned out that every group of two or three men who walked passed was likely to car jack me. It didn't really help that groups of men seemed to be getting chased off from something, that I could not see every two or three minutes. It was with great relief that we set off again, I am sure there would have been no problem anyway it was just blind paranoia.

We had a lunch stop off at Bloukrans, which at 216 metres then boasted the highest bungee jump in the world. We watched a couple jump, they must have been mad to do it anyway AND pay for the privilege!

We soon got to Plettenberg Bay and into our room at the Whale Song Coastal Lodge, it was very nice and we liked the thatched roof. Our room also had a good look over the bay towards the Tsitsikamma mountain range. The only downside was its closeness to the N2 motorway junction, the plus side was it was easy for us to get back on that same road to George in the morning. We decided to have a scout into town to find the 'Look-out' which had been recommended to us. We found it quite easily and parked up the car just to have a look at the menu. There was a lady near to the cars who was obviously looking after them in an ad hoc sort of way.

I also wondered whether those young lads around football grounds in my youth actually did 'Look after yer car mister'.

This in turn reminded me of a joke by Bernard Manning when he parked his car near to Anfield;

'Look after yer car mister?' says the young lad. To which Manning replies;

'I have got a Rottweiler in that car why would I need someone to look after it?', to which the lad says;

'Can the dog put out fires?', enough said.

The menu looked great so we went back to the car and I gave the lady what change I had, I don't think it was enough as a number of what appeared to be heated Xhosa clicks followed us as we got back in the car. A quick change at the hotel saw us back to the 'Look-out' by taxi for a few sundowners, it was chilly but the view was great, as was the place. We had Kingklip and Snoek in our two-course meal and the whole thing including drinks was less than £10. They even provided electric blankets as the temperature dipped! Our taxi driver had moved to the area from Pretoria because it was such a great place. We had to agree although we had not seen a lot. The taxi fare return was also well under £10 so we had another great and inexpensive night out.

The sunset behind the mountains was spectacular, a bright orange, set behind the black silhouette of the mountains falling down into the sparkle coming off the sea. That sounds a bit poetic but it was very spectacular. Up early the next day, we had a tremendous breakfast cooked to order then headed off down the N2 towards George. We stopped at Knysya and Wilderness on our way through and we were not disappointed when we got to the Fancourt resort just outside George sitting underneath the Outinequa mountain range. The price that we had arranged with the hotel was pretty good when compared to other Golf resorts that we had stayed at for example, Pebble Beach, Gleneagles and Turnberry. In fact, it was unbelievable. We had got a room, dinner, bed and breakfast with a game of golf for Lisa and two games for me for about a third of the price of the aforementioned venues. The setting was just as good, as were the courses, the staff, the rooms and the food. Our car was even valet parked, and our room upgraded at no extra cost. The only downside was that the 'Links' course, where the Presidents Cup had been played, was closed, other than that it was brilliant.

It was now the Saturday of the third test match so we had to play golf and get to a TV in the bar before kick off in the afternoon. Our room was not ready but we had come ready to play golf so off we went to the Montagu course with our caddy Karl, who informed me that he had caddied for Ernie Els for the last seventeen years when he had visited the estate. The course itself was very nice with houses and apartments spread around, the back drop of the mountains and the sunshine made it even more enjoyable and above all it was quiet. The greens were 10.5 on the stimpometer and they had been hollow tyned. Despite an enforced stay at the half way house (which appears to be normal practice in South Africa, i.e. you pay for a voucher for the caddy who goes off to his own area) we whizzed round, got into our room and changed ready for the match.

Gerald who appeared to be in charge of the valet parking made a huge fuss about my 2005 Lions top as we entered the hotel, and there were a few Bok grimaces as we took our seats. It didn't need a lot of beer for me to be shouting at the TV and I showed great elation when Shane scored the first try, this went into overdrive when he went over the second time. I especially loved the total commitment of Flutey in getting to the bouncing ball and flicking it to Shane. We were playing great in another physical match and I for one, with the beer in the hotel at pub prices and the great free snacks, was loving every minute of it.

At half time, there was no shortage of Africaan mutterings coming our way and it wasn't very welcoming from its tone. The second half was a lot closer, although another Lions try from Monye, much again to my loud delight, saw the Lions run out deserving 28 – 9 winners. There was no way that we deserved to be beaten 3 – 0 and there was elation at the stadium, which was once again red, as well as in my own little Lions corner of the garden route. Lisa although not as loud was very pleased as well. It was the first Lions test win since the first test against Australia in 2001, I was made up for Stubby, Mace and Matthew who had seen them all, a great end to their trip. Ours however was far from finished. In fairness most of the South Africans present, especially Mark, a Natal Sharks fan congratulated us. Gerald appeared to be overjoyed and made a number of comments about my 2005 Lions top, the reason why I keep saying that will be apparent.

We went for a quick swim after the game and made a mistake by going into the family pool. Over exuberantly I started playing ball with the kids, one of whose parents was not very pleased when the small ball rattled against her child's head. The moral to the tale, as always is do not swim when intoxicated, we left under somewhat of a cloud! Lisa was laughing her head off, no one got hurt in fairness.

Back at the room, the travel iron was playing up but soon got fixed and we changed for a meal at the Cantina restaurant, which was good as was the Rose wine. Mark was there but didn't see us as he was that inebriated! I also discovered that Lisa had grasped the Xhosa dialect or was she tutting? All in all it had been a great day!

The sun shone again the next day and we ate breakfast overlooking the first hole of the Outinequa course. I was playing, Lisa was going to the Spa. The breakfast selection was excellent and I met up with Karl just in time to smote one off the first under the withering glance of Lisa. We were first out so it was very much millionaires golf. Karl pointed out Justin Rose's mum's house and also that of the late Hanse Cronje. Some of the holes were spectacular and an 82 was not a bad result at all for a first go at the course. The mountain range looked stunning and I was looking forward to a drive through it that afternoon.

A change back at the room into the 2009 Lions t-shirt again drew comments from Gerald and we drove off towards the mountains. The Outinequa pass was stunning and a little like ripples of water coming down from a great height, but these ripples were set in the rocks. The shadows which they gave off just added to our viewing pleasure. At the bottom as we drove towards Oudsthoorn there were fields and fields of ostriches, it was their skin, which

was the purpose of our trip. .

I had seen a South African travel programme that mentioned the 'mermaids of the Karoo' and a connection to near Oudsthoorn where 'San' paintings had been found in a cave.

The 'Bushmen' or 'San' people are the oldest inhabitants of Southern Africa, where they have lived for at least 20,000 years. Their home is in the vast expanse of the Kalahari desert. There are many different

Bushman peoples - they have no collective name for themselves, and the terms 'Bushman', 'San', 'Basarwa' (in Botswana) and so on are used variously

I had e-mailed a lady who may have got us access to the cave which was in a very remote location. She had kindly said that we could ring her when we were nearer to her address out in the sticks. Unfortunately, as we drove I could see that we had some miles to go and I didn't fancy a run over the pass in the dark if I am honest, so we left it.

This was a shame as the story is a nice one;

The Karoo is a vast semi-desert area divided into the Groot Karoo and Klein Karoo of the south, where many a local claim to have spotted a mermaid combing her hair alongside a mountain rock pool.

One popular story is that of a Mermaid who has been seen at waterfalls and rivers all over the Karoo. With children warned not to go near deep pools, in case the Water-maid or Water-auntie drags them in, talk of the Karoo Mermaid is still very much alive today.

Many Klein Karoo residents have reported seeing a mysterious woman with blue eyes, pink cheeks and a fish-tail, lounging beside deep mountain pools. She simply sits and combs her long black hair before disappearing and leaving you to question your sanity.

Over 250 million years ago, the Klein Karoo was not the desert that it is today, but rather a world that existed under the sea.

San rock paintings located in the driest of Karoo areas depict Mermaid-like creatures, suggesting that she has been around for longer than any of us can comprehend. The San people were known for directly depicting what they saw, not interpretive rituals. The Mermaid images were also often shown to be holding something, convincing many that they had arms and not wings, implying that these were creatures encountered and recorded by the San people.

In 1875, a farmer named Mr D Ballot from Molensrivier recorded a story told to him by an elderly bushman. This bushman spoke of spirits that lived under the water at Eseljagtspoort near Oudtshoorn and took the form of women or animals and were believed to grab anyone who passed by and drown them in the watery abyss.

In Prince Albert stories abound about people who go swimming in the pool at Meiringspoort sometimes return to find their clothes have disappeared, mischievously removed by the Mermaid.

On our arrival into Oudsthoorn we discovered that Sunday was very much Sunday and everywhere, apart from the Kentucky, which we had for dinner, was closed. We even drove to quite a remote ostrich leather farm, that was also shut, so in more glorious sunshine we gave ourselves another stunning view of the pass and went back to the hotel. I am glad really, I quite liked the strange animals anyway.

Gerald met us to sort out the car, and due to his continued interest in the Lions tops I promised to send him one when I got home. He was elated and promised to give me his details before we left in the morning. I then thought that it would be a good idea to get hold of a golf buggy to have a drive around the estate. I wanted to see the Links course as it was closed for refurbishment. The pro shop fixed us up at a small cost and off we went…ish there was not much juice in the battery. Our trip across the courses and over to the links consisted of coasting down hills and going very slowly up the other side. To be honest apart from the wildlife there was not much to see at the Links but it was a nice afternoon…apart from the buggy. It really started playing up when we were miles from the pro shop and now consisted of me pushing it up hills with Lisa steering and laughing all at the same time. Downhill was easy until I gave up this Shackleton like expedition and called up the shop from a handy phone. They took ages to come out to us so we abandoned our ride and walked back to the shop to let them know where it was.

The rose wine back in the room went down well and it was then off to the bar for a sundowner watching a cloud lying half way up a mountain called Craddock, or a cloud called Craddock I can't remember which. It was all very nice. This time we chose to use the adults pool in the spa and no one got hurt. At night we went to the

Fish restaurant for Kingklip and Sole, and a laughing waitress who could see my delight at the quantity of chocolate in the pudding.

I was quite fuzzy the next morning when the phone rang at 7.20am, it was Gerald just making sure we didn't go before getting his address. So we were up early ish anyway, we went for breakfast and checked out, only to discover that Gerald had our car key held captive. The blokes at the main entrance told us he had just taken a family off to a room. Not for long he hadn't because before we could draw breath he was back to where we were with the family in tow still waiting to be taken to their room. They were all still on the buggy. Gerald gave me his details and we set off for Hermanus. I sent the shirt when I got home and am very pleased to say Fancourt confirmed its arrival to a very pleased Gerald. Hope he wears it in 2021.I will be checking.

We stopped off briefly at Mossel Bay on the way to Hermanus which was nice in parts then we had quite an uneventful trip into Hermanus. Once we got there the first person we spoke to was in effect our new landlady. We were driving up a street when this car stopped and a lady got out to ask if I was Mr Goodwin. I was amazed, she said that she was just on her way out and we looked lost so she thought we may be her guests. She owned two guest houses and we were put into Les Baleines, which I have to say was absolutely stunning and very much a five-star guest house, with common rooms overlooking the bay. We had a very brief nose around then headed straight out as we had come to see the whales. It was a little early in the season but we knew that whales had already been sighted so we were hoping to get lucky.

The southern right whale (Eubalaena australis) is a baleen whale, one of three species classified as right whales belonging to the genus Eubalaena. Like other right whales, the southern right whale is readily distinguished from others by the callosities on its head, a broad back without a dorsal fin, and a long arching mouth that begins above the eye. Its skin is very dark grey or black, occasionally with some white patches on the belly. The right whale's callosities appear white due to large colonies of cyamids (whale lice). It is almost indistinguishable from the closely related North Atlantic and the North Pacific right whales, displaying only minor skull differences. It may have fewer callosities on its head and more on its lower lips than the two northern species Approximately 12,000 southern right whales are spread throughout the southern part of the Southern Hemisphere. They are called 'Right' because whalers considered them the 'right' whales to hunt.

I had a map with a number of viewing points on it, but we tried the harbour first without any joy. We then drove along the coast for quite some time, again without any luck. I then drove us down a dirt road towards the sea, which led us into the local township. Before we knew it, we were surrounded by shanty buildings, dust everywhere, people everywhere and dogs wherever you looked. Advice we had been given was to only enter the townships with a guide. We didn't have one, so with the greatest respect to the locals headed quickly back to the main road, I am sure that we would have been fine but we had followed all the advice up to this point and been okay, no need to ignore it now.

We then found and parked up at a place called 'Boiling Point' it was like a headland to the west of the main town. As we walked towards the sea I spotted something in the water near to some canoeists, when I took a longer look I could see it was a whale. I shouted to Lisa and have to say that I started crying. It was an uplifting moment, not many people get to see whales in the wild. We had come here specifically to see them and had got very very lucky so early in the season.

I had never seen a whale at sea before, despite being in the Royal Navy for six years. It was without doubt the most beautiful thing I had ever seen. The whale dived and I got video of its' tail entering the water; it was brilliant and we were able to watch it dive and surface for quite some time, we even saw another one not far away. The canoeists seemed, initially oblivious to their presence, then looked like they were trying to follow them. We moved to a couple of other sites and saw whales again, we were not sure if they were the same ones. It was an amazing experience well worth the drive and visit to Hermanus.

We stopped off at a store on the way back for more rose wine. Once back at Les Baleines we tried to spy more whales from the balcony with the binoculars provided for the purpose, no luck this time. We booked a taxi into town. Our taxi driver Francois was a brilliant guide recommending pubs and a restaurant and even telling us that our local (to the hotel) baboon troop had lost their leader who had been shot by 'some idiot from the mountains behind the town. As he dropped us off at Cubana he pointed out two whale calves swimming in the dusk down in the cove. What a great finish to our whale watching for the day.

The town was quite small but we found the Zebra bar and a pub called Bo Jangles which did the job before we went back to eat at Cubana, where a Kir Royale cocktail was the princely sum of about £2. We had ribs, lamb and steak and sat watching the full moon shining over the whales and the Ocean. We got a taxi back with Francois, whose surname was Jones, I never did ask him why and we discovered an 'honesty' bar. We had for once had enough so did not partake on this occasion.

In the morning I have to say we were a little sad at leaving Hermanus so soon. The breakfast was tremendous, think of everything healthy then double it, then add in some homemade baking.

Our drive to Cape Town was to be along the coast with some stops on the way, the scenery for this last long leg of our trip was at times breathtaking. We stopped first at Betty's Bay where there was a large colony of African penguins who were funny in the extreme, especially as you can get so close to them.

The African Penguin is found on the south-western coast of Africa. It is also known as the Jackass Penguin for its donkey-like bray, although several species of South American penguins produce the same sound. It is the only penguin species that breeds in Africa and its presence gave the name to the Penguin Islands.

We saw another whale in a bay along the coast and jaw dropped our way along the road around False Bay.

The name "False Bay" was applied early on (at least three hundred years ago) by sailors who confused the bay with Table Bay to the north. The confusion arose because sailors returning from the east (The Dutch East Indies) initially confused Cape Point and Cape Hangklip, which are somewhat similar in form.

This has to be one of the most stunning drives in the world, and we had the pleasure under blue skies with time to spare, the word spectacular does it a discredit. Our directions into Cape Town and to our hotel were spot on and we found it no problem, although coming from this direction you do hit the city from the wrong direction for the classic Table Mountain view. For that you would really need to come in from the sea with Robben Island behind you, but I am certainly no expert at all.

Chapter 16
Cape Town and home

Our hotel was a 'boutique' type very similar to 'Les Baleines', I parked outside and walked in through the open door.... then fell through the floor. The floorboards behind the door had been lifted for some maintenance and the warning sign forgotten. Had I not have been going slow then a broken leg would have been the least of my worries. I extricated myself and went to check in, the staff were great, the room was lovely and the bloke who looked after the cars outside a top man.

We had a quick turnaround then it was off for a game of Golf at Rondebosch. The directions were a bit iffy but we found it soon enough. A member at my Golf Club had been a member here some years before. I paid the fee, got a cart and went off to the first tee to be informed that we were behind a ladies competition. No problem I thought, the sun is shining we are right underneath Table Mountain and we can take our time. More appropriately the ladies could steal our time! At our club I find the ladies play more quickly than the men, not at this club. We started on the 9th hole and had played the back nine three hours later. Three hours I ask you for ten holes, that in anyone's book is ridiculous. The marshall who was a Brit kept coming to us to tell us how slow they were but this was a joke. Brian, who was the club director or similar, even came to me on the first tee to apologise for my being given this tee time and offered another round, another day. I said I could not play again, but fair play the offer still stands now as far as I am aware. The light was falling by the time we got to the 6th, there were a lot of players behind us at that time, but we called it a day, so missed three holes. There was no way anyone behind us or several (including the ladies) in front would have got in, that is the cost of slow play it ruins peoples rounds. If you want to play slowly fine, but don't impose it on everyone else, and there is nothing anywhere that says you can't let people through if you are playing a competition. The course itself was not bad at all with some good use of a man made waterway on the back nine, the front being more pleasing on the eye. The 18th a short par four up the hill was probably my favourite. Maybe I will go back for that game one day.

Our drive back to the hotel was easy enough and we had a quick change before heading down to the Victoria and Alfred waterfront development by taxi. It is a nice place to stroll around for a few drinks and we decided to at last try the 'Spur' steak and grill restaurant chain for food. It was a good choice, a free salad bar, drinks licence, T-bone steak and a cheeseburger went down very well. We stumbled upon the Ferrymans Tavern as featured in Invictus to round off the night then got a taxi back.

At the hotel in the lounge was a Scottish couple, Ian and Carole from Edinburgh. They were both teachers who had been working with children in Zululand where they had been several times, and were now rounding off their visit. Nice people. We finished off with a nice complimentary drink and a couple of homemade biscuits.

Unfortunately our room although very nice was near to the back door where the staff and tradesmen entered. This woke us up pretty early but we had slept well anyway. It was another nice morning and we could look up and see Table Mountain from a small court yard attached to our room. Breakfast was excellent and we were soon met by Marlene from African Eagle tours who was to be our guide for the day on our 'Best of Cape Town' tour. We were joined by Rachel and a friend from Manchester, an architect from Johannesburg, a Japanese couple, an Irish lady called Megan and an Australian family from Perth whose son or daughter was marrying a South African, much to the glee of Marlene who foresaw some interesting times watching rugby and cricket games between the two. Marlene was a great guide.

Our first stop was Camp's Bay where we had a great view of the twelve apostles, which is a range of hills sitting sort of to the west of Table mountain overlooking Camp Bay facing out towards the South Atlantic. On a sunny day like this they looked fantastic and the camera clickers were soon on high alert. The Cape was actually a lot bigger than I thought. We made our way through Constantia, where Mark Thatcher lived to Fish Hoek (corner), Simonstown and Seaforth where there was a great penguin colony that we stopped off to see. At one stage we stopped on what now was the east side of the Cape, overlooking False Bay. There, Marlene pointed out the coast card who was effectively looking for Great White Sharks. She told us the tale of a local lady aged 75 years who had swum every morning in the bay for many years, until one morning her luck ran out and all that was left was her bathing cap. If you are ever considering swimming where they may be sharks here are some handy tips;

Do not swim, surf or surf/ski when birds, dolphins or seals are feeding nearby.

Do not swim, surf or surf/ski near where trek-netting, fishing or spear fishing is taking place.

Do not swim in deep water beyond the breakers.

Do not swim if you are bleeding.

Do not swim near river mouths.

Do not swim, surf or surf/ski at night.

Do not swim, surf or surf/ski if there has been a cetacean stranding nearby.

If a shark has recently been sighted in an area where no shark spotters are present, consider using another beach for the day.

First time visitors to beach areas should ask the local law enforcement official, life guards or locals about the area.

Obey beach officials if told to leave the water.

For those people kayaking or surf/skiing far out to the sea, consider paddling in groups and staying close together (in a diamond shape).

Consider using a personal shark shield when you go surfing or kayaking.

Pay attention to any shark signage on beaches.

Hope that helps!

We travelled on to the Cape which had been first sailed past, well by a non-local anyway, by Bartolomeu Dias a Portuguese sailor in search of a route to India. Vasco de Gama later made it all the way to India and there is a religious monument to him on the Cape. It was a great sunny day and the point of Good Hope was busy but we made it to the top and did the picture touristy thing, as you do. From here we made our way back north to Muizenberg which had some very interesting historical significance;

The Battle of Muizenberg was a small but significant military affair that began in June 1795 and ended three months later with the (first) British occupation of the

Cape. Thus, began the period (briefly interrupted from 1804 to 1806) of British control of the Cape, and subsequently much of Southern Africa. The historical remnant of the Battle of Muizenberg is a site on the hillside overlooking False Bay that holds the remains of a defensive fort started by the Dutch in 1795 and expanded by the British from 1796 onwards.

Rhodes' Cottage is also in Muizenberg a small house on the seafront that Cecil John Rhodes, the 'founder' of modern day Zimbabwe ex Rhodesia, bought as a holiday cottage and this was where he died in 1902. The house is preserved as a museum dedicated to Rhodes' life and is open to the public.

Marlene also told us that Rhodes and Rudyard Kipling had once walked together on the beach, and that the place was mentioned in his poem the 'Flowers' and she was right;

Buy my English posies!
Here's to match your need--
Buy a tuft of royal heath,
Buy a bunch of weed
White as sand of Muysenberg
Spun before the gale--
Buy my heath and lilies
And I'll tell you whence you hail!
Under hot Constantia broad the vineyards lie--

Throned and thorned the aching berg props the speckless sky--
Slow below the Wynberg firs trails the tilted wain--
Take the flower arid turn the hour, and kiss your love again!

At this juncture, some of our fellow passengers who were on a half day trip left us, the rest of us including Rachel and her friend moved onto Stellenbosch and the wine regions. I liked Stellenbosch it was a white building type of place, with a University which was 40/60 Africaans, we had some lunch and a walk around the market, where a black guy said he loved my shoes! They were only Reebok walking ones and if I had brought another pair with me he could have had them. But I hadn't, so he couldn't.

We then set off for the Zevenwacht wine tasting experience. We had never done one and I found the it to be very good, I had a slight problem with our guide whose first name was Morne, it took me back to Pretoria but he was nice enough. I learned that it wasn't about the colour of the grape but how long it stayed in the vat as to whether it was white, red or rose. The tasting was also good and I have now learnt to savour wine as opposed to thinking it was a race to drink it the fastest. I also learnt that Pinotage is solely South African. There were also cheeses to try, which was a nice touch, so we spent a few quid in the shop including, amongst the wine, a toy Rhino for Euan. Which is now Ronnie and very well used too. It had been a long day as we headed back to town and the girls fell asleep, so missing the sight of Cape Flats Township which for size has to be seen to be believed. Marlene told us of foreign workers who came in to erect brick built accommodation to replace the corrugated steel buildings, which was a charitable function. However, she also pointed out that a lot of the brick buildings now had extensions in the form of rickety corrugated iron.

To be honest my views on the life of the indigenous South Africans would take another book, but twenty years after majority rule returned the plight of millions really is quite heart breaking. There are very many successful black people in South Africa and there did seem to be a real concern that there was a financial and 'brain' drain going on in relation to a lot of whites who were needed in the country. Conversely a lot of white people told me that they had real concerns that South Africa would be the next Zimbabwe which anyone can see has been completely ruined by the despot Mugabe. Once again the pendulum has been pulled back not to equilibrium, as it should be, but to another extreme which in no way counters the first.

I will move on, once back at the Cape Cadogan, as it was our last night we went straight out, this time being confident enough to have a walk down Kloof and Long Street. We stopped at a few bars on the way down, and were only approached by one young lad who was after, and later got some change from us. I did notice an African restaurant to our right as we walked.

It advertised African game which we thought would be a good finish. When we were hungry we made our way back towards it but couldn't find it and nearly ended up back at the hotel. We walked back down again and came across Khaya Myama, which was a great find. We had ostrich, crocodile, eland, kudu and warthog and loved it all. The bill as always was very competitive and it was a great finish to our African eating although the holiday wasn't yet over. Back at the hotel complimentary chocolate was joined with a few more beers, Ashes cricket and we had a result.

Lisa is not really one for heights, neither, if I am honest, am I. However as our flight was later that day we had time in the morning to go up Table Mountain on the cable car. Lisa said she would have a look before deciding. We drove and parked up, it was a gorgeous day, not a cloud in the sky….so we went for it. The cable cars in 2009 were extremely modern compared to the old ones, which looked very very dodgy. I have to say the views from the car and across the city were tremendous, the wind over the top of the mountain quite surprising, we did not see any baboons. Lisa looked down at the floor all the way up and all the way down. The dodgy bit for me was nearing the top when you think that you cannot miss the rocks of the mountain. I couldn't help but look out, not only to film, but because it felt like being in a plane where I can't resist looking out, when others would rather not. Overall it was a great experience and we were glad that we had the good fortune to do it.

We still had a little time left so went to the District 6 museum. This for me summed up the whole issue of South Africa and its history. It was a moving exhibition with some sad and uplifting tales. For example the man who kept homing pigeons prior to being forcibly moved, only to find that despite his best efforts they kept returning to their home in District Six. I cannot imagine how it must feel like to be told you are moving from a home where you have lived for many years. Cape Flats is effectively a monument to District Six and all 'clearances' throughout the world.

On 11 February 1966, the South African government declared District Six a whites-only area under the Group Areas Act, with removals starting in 1968. By 1982, more than 60,000 people had been relocated to the sandy, bleak Cape Flats township complex some 25 kilometres away. The old houses were bulldozed. The only buildings left standing were places of worship. International and local pressure made redevelopment difficult for the government, however. The Cape Technikon (now Cape Peninsula University of Technology) was built on a portion of District Six which the government renamed Zonnebloem. Apart from this and some police housing units, the area was left undeveloped.

Since the fall of apartheid in 1994, the South African government has recognized the older claims of former residents to the area, and pledged to support rebuilding.

There are some exhibitions that everyone needs to see, and this, if you get the chance, is one of them.

Afterwards we nipped to the Green Point stadium, being built for the 2010 World Cup and saw hundreds of men waiting to find work just outside the arena.

We went back to the hotel, showered and headed off for the airport. After check-in, we still had enough rand to have a few drinks There was a group of Lions fans sitting in departures to whom I asked 'are we the only ones left?' They thought that we may be, certainly in Cape Town anyway. We flew into the sunset with Cape Town shimmering on our left, and I decided to take advantage of the Emirates beer trolley. When we got to Dubai in the morning I was merry and fell asleep before our connection to Manchester. We arrived in the afternoon sun, where my Mom picked us up, somehow managing to fall over when she nipped to the toilet. Although not badly hurt she was a little shaken, and after a brief respite and plastering up we arrived home, credit card grumbling, pockets empty but more knowledgeable than when we left.

Chapter 17
Another World Cup and a four year wait

We still needed to see that Lions win so thoughts and savings towards Australia in 2013 commenced.

In 2011 another World Cup came along, there was talk in the papers about Wales not even getting out of their group containing South Africa, Samoa, Fiji and Namibia. Having seen them at Twickenham in a warm up I thought otherwise, they should have got something out of that game. It was also noticeable that in the last twenty minutes they appeared stronger. This proved to be the case when they beat Argentina and England in subsequent games. I thought that they would get through but South Africa in the first game was crucial. Although they lost that game by a point a great odyssey for Welsh fans commenced. A hard-fought win over the Samoans led to some spectacular rugby against the Fijians and Namibians and a quarter final against the Irish.

Rhys Priestland had come from nowhere to claim the 10 shirt, Sam Warburton was making Burger, McCaw and Pocock look like equals, Faletau a revelation. They were looking good, so much so I started to make plans for a trip to New Zealand and the final. A friend of mine, Graham Hughes, had been TMO at the tournament and had assured me of a floor to sleep on, the flights were there to be had as were tickets it was all set.

Ireland were swept aside in Wellington after a terrific performance, and a poor French side beckoned in the semi – final. On the Tuesday before the semi – final, Lisa and I went to Crete on a pre-planned holiday. We were staying just outside Malia and my first task was to find a bar which would show the game. Heaven was that bar, so after checking and double checking access to the internet in the bar and nearby in order to, hopefully, book the flights after the match, we took our seats.

There were only us and two other Welsh blokes in the place, it was after all out of season. We started really well but the rest as they say is history, Warburton gets harshly sent off, and despite a heroic performance by fourteen men, we miss our kicks and get beaten 9 v 8. It was heart breaking and the only time that I have ever cried/sobbed after saving myself quite a bit of money. My credit card breathed a sigh of relief as well, it had been a great journey and where better to win the World Cup than at Twickenham anyway? Writing in 2017 this of course didn't happen, but that was another RWC odyssey for Welsh fans.

Chapter 18
The recession bites

Well if we thought the recession was bad in 2009, we had not seen anything yet, the news was bad and didn't get any better. From a personal point of view I had been through the housing slump and high inflation of the late eighties and early nineties. We had almost lost our house because of it, this was far worse, far worse.

'meet me on the wasteland later this day we'll sit and talk and hold hands maybe for there's not much else to do in this drab and colourless place'

So, begins the 1979 track from the Jam album 'Setting Sons'. It portrays a bleak outlook on life in the UK at that time, following a Winter of Discontent and an election victory by the Conservative Party under the leadership of Margaret Thatcher. It was appropriate.

The financial crisis really started to hit home I distinctly remember several things. The first was the British institution, Woolworth's closing. I can recall walking past to see the closing down signs, and being a lover of bargains like everyone else I went in to see. As soon as I walked in and saw the staff I very quickly realised that being in the shop felt a lot like picking over the bones of someone else's demise. I bought nothing and left. Shortly afterwards I had to go into Adams children's store to exchange some shoes for my grandson. It was on the verge of closing down and it was clear the liquidators were hovering around the tills. Once again, I had an awful feeling of despair for the staff and left as quickly as I could. Another was looking around our pub and hoping that everyone would be okay as talks of job cuts made the headlines.

I could count on one hand the number of pubs that I had seen close in my lifetime. This was brought into stark reality once the recession really took hold. Everywhere we look pubs are now shut. The same can be said of High Street shops, very rarely did they close. Now every town centre, even the most affluent had empty shops, and every council practices the same thing of decorating the windows with reasons as to why you should open a shop in their town.

The most heart-breaking sight for me, and it is replicated again and again is seeing shops about to shut or staff waiting in empty shops for customers. A pie shop opened in our town during this time right on the marketplace. Great location, or so you would think, but the market moved into the town centre as the marketplace was re-furbished. The shop did not last long and I cannot remember seeing one customer inside it. The shop has moved to a location in another town, I went past it one day again not one customer it, made me sad.

I cannot remember the amount of times I have wanted to cry at seeing the devastation of ordinary people due to circumstances completely beyond their control.

Sadly, libraries were under threat I have great memories of my library as a child. I saw an advertisement outside one, it read that inside there was a Big Top and children were invited in to see what it entailed and which books would be read that week. I looked in to see two members of staff inside this Big Top arranging things. It could well be that it was being prepared. My sadness at urban life saw it as two people desperately trying to encourage the use of the library in order to save it and their jobs. It was replicated in most stores and I found it so terribly and desperately sad.

There are always good stories, Woolworth's is now B and M, my favourite shop. My youngest daughter got a promotion at work and my eldest daughter had graduated as a teacher and got her first teaching job. This does not detract from sad feelings for fellow human beings, nor from the realities of being caught up in the nightmare.

Looking around our pub and hoping that everyone would be okay as talks of job cuts made the headlines.

As a Public-Sector worker with my wife I never once considered that cuts would in any way adversely affect us, as they say you don't work in the Public Sector to become a millionaire, but it's safe. Some of our friends who were self- employed did struggle, but they have hung on. Two of the regulars were made redundant but are now working again, another took voluntary redundancy and has not since found work, generally the pub as a microcosm of the workforce had been affected but not overly so.

In twenty-three years there had been many financial crises but jobs had not been lost where we worked. In 2009 a project was undertaken at work which sought new more streamlined ways of working, it was clear from the updates that this meant jobs. It also looked like these would be lost through natural wastage. It was also clear that I would be okay but that Lisa may not be. This rumbled on and still rumbles on to-day. In January 2010, Lisa was informed that her role had been moved from review under one project to review under another. That was the start of sleepless nights and almost constant worry, I would not wish it on my worst enemy. Not to be able to plan your next steps is difficult to cope with, and I have to say the system of review was not what you would have expected had this been the private sector. Had it have been the latter, then it all would have been completed a lot quicker.

A couple of weeks later the collective consultation notes showed that her role was going, this compounded the worry and the whole thing became all consuming. As did growing concerns over colleagues in the organisation. New roles were being advertised, my wife applied but was sifted at the application stage. Time began to run out and the ever-shrinking re-deployment pool beckoned, the redundancy date was set it all looked very bleak. Then we got lucky a colleague applied for and gained another role freeing up an ideal role in the redundancy pool. Lisa applied and got the role, less money yes, less responsibility yes, but a job nonetheless.

Here lies the rub of the whole thing we are thankful for the job, but you ask yourself thankful for what? Did we lend or spend the money that led to the crisis? Did we create the jobs that are now not required? Did the shop-workers, publicans or librarians? In fact, was anyone who lost jobs or saw opportunities disappear responsible for creating the jobs or creating the crisis? The answer is no, but once more it was the ordinary Joe's and Joanne's who paid the price.

As I have said there is always a positive, and in late 2011 we had it, the dates for the 2013 tour. We hadn't paid off the credit card from the last trip. This would be our third and give us the hat-trick of visits, although I have to say, Argentina will inevitably follow in the future. It has to.

Where to go and what to do, our initial plan was to take in three tests, as it would…maybe be our last tour. However when I discovered that we could do the Great Wall, Terracotta Army, Hong Kong and Australia for 40% less than going on two separate holidays, it was a no brainer and the credit card ran off. As did the chance to watch all three tests. However I have always thought that the second test is the key where it is won lost or drawn, and I was happy with our choice.

So the plan was fly to Beijing and see the wall, then to Xian for the terracotta army, into Hong Kong for a couple of nights then fly to Perth. From there we would take the 'Indian Pacific' to Adelaide and drive on the Great Ocean Road to Melbourne, take in the test match and then make the return journey from there.

Chapter 19
The game is afoot

In the summer of 2012 Ireland, Wales, England and Scotland flexed their muscles in the southern hemisphere. It would be fair to say that if I now told you Scotland beat Fiji and Samoa but lost to Australia, Ireland lost 2 v 1 against the All Blacks, England lost 2 v 1 against the Springboks and Wales beat Australia 2 v 1 or even 3 v 0, if you had watched all the matches you wouldn't have been surprised. The fact was Scotland won 3 v 0, Ireland and Wales lost 3 v 0, and England went down 2 v 0. It did not tell the whole story.

By this time I had found an old-school friend on Facebook, Craig Clayton, who now lived in Australia and in Melbourne site of the 2nd test no less. I contacted Craig to find out a few things then started the booking process. I started off with Deva in Chester who had sorted out South Africa in 2009. I have to say the service this time was poor the price went up by £2,000 from an initial quote and when I questioned this they did not re-contact. The same could be said for Kuoni who despite doing a good job in 2005 have since consistently failed to re-engage my quote requests and/or started off the process then not re-contacted.

A search on the net found Travel Bag and our agent Hugh who was brilliant from start to finish and did the whole holiday for a lot less than Deva and with some additional requests from me thrown in.

We had decided once again as it was so far that we would visit as many places as we could en route to the game so the itinerary looked a bit like this:

Heathrow flight to Beijing to visit the Great Wall, then a flight to Xian to see the Terracotta Army followed by a couple of nights in Hong Kong. We would then fly to Australia and have a couple of days in Perth followed by the 'Indian Pacific' train across the desert and outback to Adelaide where after a short break we would drive down the great ocean road to Warmabool for a stop off before finishing with three days and the 2nd test in Melbourne.

As usual the tickets were causing us concerns in September 2012 as they were already appearing on Viagogo for £250 each and they weren't officially on sale. An email was sent to the Lions office to ask why this was and to ask for access to tickets at once. Again we got no reply. Craig subsequently told me that the game in Melbourne would not sell out so tickets should be easy enough to get. I was hearing of 40,000 travelling to Australia so I wasn't so sure but I did now have a foot in both camps for tickets when the time came. To cover all bets, I also enlisted the help of a former colleague Dan to see if he could buy some.

Andy Mason and Stubby had decided against touring due to the expense in Australia which was down to a strong dollar. They had done all three Lions tours and the World Cup in Australia anyway, so instead it was golf in Turkey for them.

Wales had won another Grand Slam in 2012 having watched the win in Dublin live I have to say with some bias that it was deserved. I was buoyed enough to tick off another test nation by booking to watch the Samoans in Cardiff in the autumn series. The Samoans were too good by half and the team who seemed to be working to the next level were now collapsing and short of ideas. If you had asked me to name my test fifteen for the Lions before the autumn it would have been very different to the one I now select, the date for the record is the 20th November 2012 and I am on the National Express Birmingham to Crewe 4.30pm service so here goes with the team (see how I have cleverly put you all in the now although you will be reading this years hence!). This excludes injuries I will pretend that I have a full squad. Well I have lied as I have just changed it to my post autumn international team after another heart-breaking loss for Wales against Australia.
    15. Leigh Halfpenny

14. Tommy Bowe
13. Jonathan Davies
12. Jamie Roberts
11. George North
10. Jonathan Sexton
9. Danny Care (not in original party)
8. Jamie Heaslip
7. Chris Robshaw (not in original party)
6. Dan Lydiate
5. Geoff Parling
4. Richie Grey
3. Adam Jones
2. Dylan Hartley
1. Cian Healey

We will match that against the test team in a few months!

Before I leave 2012 behind I must say that it was the best year of sport I can ever remember. It started with that Grand Slam, then Wiggins in the Tour de France, that goal by Aquero for Manchester City. Murray winning the US Open and the Olympics, McIlroy the US PGA, the Olympics, the Paralympics and then the Miracle at Medinah it just went on and on. With the Jubilee, it just showed that the Brits could step up to the mark. Lord Coe said, after the London Olympics 'When our time came we did it right'………Did it right? when our time came as a watcher, attender, volunteer, worker or athlete we absolutely nailed it, didn't we?

Favourite moment watching Victoria Pendleton winning the Keirin, in the pub, the roof came off, and everyone stood up to sing the anthem, absolutely priceless. We could not get any official tickets despite applying but we did take our grandson Euan to London on the weekend of the opening ceremony. As we couldn't get tickets the next best thing was to go to Victoria Park where there was an opening ceremony event not far from the main stadium. We queued up for hours to get in then a bloke at the entrance said we couldn't take in our video camera, bit daft given what mobiles now do. He wouldn't budge and pointed to the exit where we would have to leave. We walked that way then blended in with the 30,000 crowd and disappeared into the site, so escaping justice! In the site we went on the big wheel and got in front of the screen. The atmosphere was fantastic, the Red Arrows came over and the biggest cheer was saved for the Queen when she turned to speak to James Bond, if there had have been a roof it would have come off. Euan waved his little Union Jack flag at the appropriate moments but he was tired so with the countries at C we left. By the time we had walked across the park, taken the train to Honor Oak Park, picked our car up from near my daughter Laura's house and driven for twenty minutes, Team GB came into the stadium. I also must say that as we walked past my daughter Laura's flat there was some proper noise coming from in there. The next day we went back into London and saw the cycling road race come through

Knightsbridge, apparently, part of the biggest ever Olympic crowd in doing so. We had done our bit. 2012 was a stellar year to be a Brit.

In January 2013, the following article appeared in the Metro written by Tariq Tahir, this together with the work of Sharon Hodgson MP on the general UK ticket fiasco would rattle a few cages.

British and Irish rugby fans' bank balances will face a mauling if they want to see the Lions tour Australia this summer, a watchdog has warned.

While the home support will be able to snap up seats for the three test matches at £61 a pop, Lions followers are being forced to buy them as part of an official travel package costing a minimum of £2,499 for all the tests.

Even throwing in a replica shirt worth £55 shouldn't sweeten the deal, which? says, as accommodation isn't included.

The magazine's article says: 'If it was possible to buy in person, it would actually be cheaper to fly to Australia in February to buy tickets, and then fly back again for the matches, rather than buy the official package.'

Which? adds that, for a total of £1,165, a Lions fan could ask an Australian friend to buy them three tickets and take a return flight plus flights between cities hosting the matches.

Justin Hopwood, of Lions Rugby Travel, defended the ticket policy, saying: 'There is a range of ticket options to choose from, and we strongly believe the official packages represent value for money when compared to other major sporting events.'

However, Which? accused the company of ripping off fans, adding: 'British and Irish Lions Ltd should sell tickets at face value prices to their supporters, exactly as the Australians do, and in the same way organisers of the rugby and football world cups do.

I emailed the story far and wide and tweeted it and we will see what transpires, although I had by now asked two friends living in Australia to get me tickets when the sales opened on the 18th of February. Bear in mind in November 2012 they were appearing for sale on Viagogo!!!

Having registered on Ticketmaster Australia some months before, in the vain hope that I could get tickets, it had been made clear that those without a residential Australian address had to go through the aforesaid 'official' tours. Where was the Aussie sense of fair play? This time it was an even more complete stitch up than in previous years, even friends of mine who didn't really follow rugby were incredulous that to get a ticket you also had to book flights, hotels and go to destinations you didn't want to go to.

As it was we had friends in Australia a little bit like 'sleeper' spies who would try to get me tickets when they went on sale at 10pm our time on Sunday the 17th of

February, I thought I had it covered? 10pm comes on that Sunday and I thought I would just give it a try as Ticketmaster Australia had sent me an email which said my 'favourite' the Melbourne Test was coming up for purchase. So in I went…and on I went….and select four Gold tickets I want (the only ones left) and to payment I went…and to receipt I got…two! The first Lions tickets I had ever got at first point of sale for face value. It got better, the following day Dan told me he had got two standing tickets, Craig had tried but in fairness the whole lot for the test matches had sold out in fifteen minutes……again not to genuine fans as this screen shot from Viagogo will attest, posted the week that they went on sale.

VIAGOGO
Australia vs British and Irish Lions
Etihad Stadium, Saturday, 29 June 2013 18:00
Section: Gold L3 17
Number of Tickets: 2
Price: $1,333.33
Booking Fee: (Ticket Guarantee and Customer Service) $200.00
Shipping: (Based on lowest priced delivery to: United Kingdom) $53.00
VAT: $40.00

The actual price of these tickets was around $490. I could print pages of similar ones off, a black market completely created by the monopoly that is the British and Irish Lions Ltd. The practice of the home Union in Lions ticketing doesn't help a great deal either.

Back to my tickets: pretty chuffed I was and contacted Stubby who was now thinking about the last two tests to let him know he could have the standing ones if he wanted, he asked me to keep hold of them. A couple of days after this euphoria I had an email from Ticketmaster, stating that it was a 'condition of sale' that I had to supply an Australian address when buying, and that if I did not they would rescind the tickets. Fortunately, another friend sorted that out for me and I supplied it without any apparent problems. To date, the payment has gone out and the tickets are still showing as mine so fingers crossed (this was written at the end of February 2013). I could obviously fall back on the standing tickets if needed but would really have to wait until the 14th of May when tickets could be printed off to make sure that I had the seated ones. I will most certainly be going to the monopolies commission…once I have seen the match I don't trust anyone in relation to this absolute carve up which clearly now involves the ARU as well.

So to clarify if I have a non-Australian address I can't apply for tickets at a venue where I could if it was not the British and Irish Lions playing?? Isn't that a bit racist?? Maybe not but absolutely infuriating.

Let's look at it from the point of view of someone visiting our shores to go to say Wimbledon or the Open or the Boat Race.

So I am Mr Brewster from Chattanooga and I have applied for all three on my round Europe vacation....so far so good. Wimbledon let me have centre court in the ballot for day one. I get Open tickets as well but not the Boat Race. So I am really pleased with my travel agent from downtown who now tries to pay on my behalf…...

'Oh sorry your client can't have them'
'Why'
'Doesn't have a UK residential address'
'Why does he need that?'
'Because he does'
'How do we get around it?'
'Easy buy all your flights and hotels off us, we will tell you where you are going and you can have as many tickets as you want'
'Where would my client be going?'
'Apart from Muirfield and Wimbledon, Coventry, Rhyl, Motherwell and Cork'
'But he doesn't want to go there'
'You can't have the tickets then, these packages are competitively priced at around £4,000 per person'
'But we can do the trip for about 40% less than that'
'Not if you want the tickets you can't'
'Right I will get some on the black market then, they are appearing on Viagogo and Seatwave as we speak'

'Okay'

Similarly imagine your horror if you applied for a ticket at your local Rugby club to be told you can have one as long as you use our transport to get you there and do what we want you to do while you are at the ground! Utterly utterly ludicrous and I will try until my toes turn up to get it sorted. It will have to wait, don't want to get black listed do I.

An email to the Rugby Club on Sky Sports got no airing, shame on them, it is we privateers that make Lions tours what they are or have become and without us there would not be 30,000 people at the venues. Paul Ackford who I think I have mentioned before did have an opinion…...thanks Paul, about the only one who would put it in print.

I will move on.

Chapter 20
The forgotten tours?

It has occurred to me in recent weeks that the talk of the Lions largely centres around the 71, 74 tours then 89 onwards. There is very little in the way of conversation about the tours in between so I thought that this would be a good point to bridge that gap.

1977 – The Lions found it was payback time. Phil Bennett led the side who were coached by John Dawes and managed by the Scot George Burrell. They lost the series 3 – 1. The backs included legends like Andy Irvine, Mike Gibson, Ian McGeechan and JJ Williams in addition to the great Phil Bennett. The pack included Fran Cotton, Peter Wheeler, Graham Price, Bill Beaumont, Gordon Brown, Terry Cobner and Willie Duggan.

Despite a focus on forward play and the emergence of a siege mentality in the face of a hostile press and one of the wettest New Zealand winters ever, the Lions lost just one of their 21 provincial games and might have drawn the Test series at the very least.

The tourists made an encouraging start to the first Test, but the double blow of a disputed try by Brad Johnstone and a 60-yard interception score by Grant Batty just before the break left them too much to do into the Wellington wind in the second half. The interval score line of 16-12 to New Zealand was unchanged at the final whistle.

The second Test was punctuated by acts of violence but it was the Lions who emerged standing, having squared the series with a 13-9 success thanks to a JJ Williams try and three Bennett penalties.

In the third, New Zealand scored three tries to one inside the first quarter of an hour and, with the Lions missing six of their seven kicks at goal, the hosts went on to a deserved 19-7 win. The fourth Test saw the tourists so dominant up front that the All Blacks were reduced to resorting to a three-man scrum, but again the visitors lost a match they should have won, conceding the decisive try in a 10-9 defeat deep into injury time.

A stopover in Fiji did little to ease the pain, particularly as the Test there was lost 25-21.

1980 – Bill Beaumont fresh from an England Grand Slam captained the side.

The tour went ahead in the face of opposition from the British Government and groups opposed to sporting contact with the apartheid regime in South Africa.

Of the 30 players originally selected, ten had previous Lions tour experience. The squad also contained a certain Clive Woodward. The tour party was disrupted by an unusually high number of injuries and replacements throughout the 10-week long tour. Eight players flew to South Africa to reinforce the original 30 tourists.

The series was lost 3 v 1 although the Lions did win all of their non-international games, including one played in modern day Namibia.

1983 – The Lions joined the 1966 side as the second team to suffer a 4-0 whitewash in the Tests.

The side captained by Ireland's Triple Crown winner Ciaran Fitzgerald, coached by two times Lions tourist Jim Telfer and managed by Willie John McBride.

The All Blacks were an impressive team, who had both a quality pack and an abundance of scoring potential out wide. Nevertheless, the Lions gave them a game.

The opening international was close, the All Blacks scoring the only try to win 16-12.

In the second Test, the Lions looked clear favourites conceding only nine first-half points whilst playing into the teeth of a Wellington gale. But with the wind in their favour, they failed to convert possession into points and fell to a masterclass in playing the conditions, losing by the interval score of 9-0.

Fitzgerald's team actually outscored the All Blacks by two tries to one in the third Test but were still edged out 15-8, before being blown away by an outstanding attacking performance that saw the hosts win the final international 38-6.

A six-year hiatus then followed largely due to their being no tour to South Africa and of course, Australia had now put their hands up as a proper Test nation and had to be included, what price Argentina in the future?

Chapter 21
The run to take off

6th of March 2013 and the requirement to pay the rest of our holiday off comes, that wakes you up and makes you start thinking about it. The Six Nations still has two games to run and is probably one of the best for years with the French losing their first three games, England hoping for a slam and Wales and Scotland right in the mix. Lions talk abounds. We had had a slight change to our itinerary as the Hong Kong to Perth flight had been cancelled, basically due to Emirates out doing Quantas and the latter having to put in with them or go bust. As a result they had cancelled some routes. Our first alternative was to go to Perth via Sydney, we didn't like this idea as effectively we would be heading in the wrong direction, face fifteen hours in the air instead of eight and lose time on our holiday. So I told Hugh that this was not an option and if we could not get to Perth more direct then we would have to change to Sydney, a road trip to Adelaide and then revert to the plan. This would have been a shame as we would miss the train trip.

I was buoyed when at my suggestion, they looked at getting us via Singapore which worked and also meant we would fly to Perth in the day and not at night so gaining more time in Perth. I was further buoyed when Hugh told me that our basic drinks…including the alcoholic ones were included on the train.

The end of the Six Nations was climactic, the Irish beaten in Rome, which is brilliant for the Six Nations, Scotland running France close…and of course that game in Cardiff. The first forty minutes reminded me very much of Pretoria 2009, it was ferocious with no one giving way at all although Wales did get the ascendency in the scrum. Some would say courtesy of Steve Walsh. In the second half the Welsh put on the afterburners and the score line became quite a shock, but deserved for Wales. England in fairness never got their heads down they were just beaten all over the park on the day. A day of days for the Welsh.

I did say my post Autumn international team should go up against the actual first test selection, but after an enthralling Six Nations I have had another go and picked a squad, first test team and a bench. Bold will denote any successes in either the squad, team or bench.

Props;
Cian Healey, Gethin Jenkins, Adam Jones, Dan Cole.

Hookers;
Richard Hibbard, Rory Best, **Tom Youngs**

Locks;
Alun Wynn-Jones, Geoff Parling, Richie Grey, Ian Evans

Back row;
Sam Warburton, Toby Faletau, Chris Robshaw, Tom Wood, **Tom Croft, Justin Tipuric**

Scrum Halfs;
Mike Phillips, Danny Care, **Ben Youngs**

Fly Halfs;
Jonathan Sexton, Owen Farrell, Dan Biggar

Centres;
Brian O'Driscoll, Jamie Roberts, Manu Tulilagi, Jonathan Davies

Wings;
George North, Alex Cuthbert, Tommy Bowe, Simon Szebo

Full Backs;
Leigh Halfpenny, Stuart Hogg

Utility Forward;
Ryan Jones

Utility Back;
James Hook
17 Welshmen, 10 Englishmen, 6 Irishmen, 2 Scotsmen

1st Test Team
1. Cian Healey
2. Richard Hibbard
3. Adam Jones
4. Alun Wynn-Jones
5. Geoff Parling
6. Sam Warburton ©
7. **JUSTIN TIPURIC**
8. Taulupe Faletau
9. Mike Phillips
10. Jonathan Sexton
11. George North
12. **JAMIE ROBERTS**
13. Manu Tuilagi
14. Leigh Halfpenny
15. Stuart Hogg

Replacements – Rory Best, Gethin Jenkins, Richie Grey, Chris Robshaw, **JAMES HOOK,** Danny Care, **SIMON SZEBO.**

Perhaps some explanation would assist the reader here. Cian Healey probably carries a little better than Gethin Jenkins, despite his disciplinary flaws. Gethin can cover both sides of the scrum. Hibbard has got better and better over the last twelve months, where Best in the Six Nations went backwards in a struggling team. Adam Jones is the best tighthead in the world. Alun Wynn – Jones gives a huge physical presence whilst Parling is great at the line out and had a good tournament. Richie Grey provides impact off the bench. Sam Warburton and Justin Tipuric showed in the second half against Scotland and against England what a destructive force they can be at the breakdown, defensively and on the front foot. Warburton gets the captaincy as a result. Robshaw can cover the back row off the bench if needed. Taulupe Faletau gets better and better and is a shoe in. Mike Phillips the scrum half who could be a back rower is too physical to leave out and Sexton has to play if fit. Centre wise I think that the God who is BOD has just too many games under his belt now and looks to always be carrying an injury these days. Roberts is good defensively which should unleash Tuilagi offensively. How do you leave Cuthbert out? Because Halfpenny has to play and Hogg gives that little bit of something else on the front foot. George North is a shoe in. Backs replacement wise Care would give me a totally different option to Phillips if required, Szebo a bit more flair to go with the bash, whilst James Hook takes care of fly half, centre or full back.

However I have highlighted in **CAPITALS** who I don't think will be in the first test team or on the bench in Brisbane! NB - As it turned out two were not in the original party!

30th April the tour squad is announced, I was in Somerset and there were a few surprises. For example, Matt Stevens got on the plane and Johnny decided his body couldn't take it despite a great display against Saracens in the Heineken Cup the weekend before. Those who I felt were unlucky not to go were Robshaw, Best, Ryan Jones and James Hook. However they may all feature in the end but let's hope that the party stays injury free. Sam Warburton is captain and in fairness as Warren Gatland said he is the most successful Northern Hemisphere captain of the last two years. I would have preferred that he concentrated on his game as he had done so effectively against Scotland and England. However it is a heavyweight team and looks like Australia are to be beaten into submission. They at the same time had their own problems with Beale and Cooper at that time out of the reckoning squad wise. It is no game afoot, can't wait for the Lions adverts.

On the holiday front I had noticed that our Australian hotels were all room only which was fine except that we had chosen Robinsons in the City in Melbourne largely because it was sited in an old bakery but also because it highlighted breakfast as a feature. Even going so far as saying that it was included in the price? I sent a query to confirm and may have changed this hotel further down the pages.

Thankfully, Paul from Robinson's found my emails querying and as I had contacted him before my tour company booked. He agreed that he would include breakfast. I am not a big breakfast eater but Lisa is and it seemed to be part of the experience so I was glad of his help. It turned out that we had also got bed and breakfast in Perth.

As a bit of a bonus Simon Reeve's new documentary Australia also started screening and it pretty much went backwards from where we were going. He started on the Indian Pacific, stopped off at Kalgoorlie and then drove to Perth. From there he went to our old haunts of Darwin and Cairns, before ending up in Melbourne after a stop in Sydney. Stuff like this before you go on holiday really wets the appetite doesn't it. It was the same when I watched the Butlin's Story on BBC having just booked to take Euan in August to their site at Skegness. This turned out inspired so much to do for a five-year-old, highly recommended.

In May, we received even more annoyance over what was quickly becoming the ticket fiasco. I had an email to say that the ARU had requested that Ticketmaster should not allow ticketholders to print off their tickets. This somewhat foiled my plans as Dan was going to transfer his to me I could then sell them before we left for what I paid and be sorted; as it was it now complicated matters. Why did the ARU do this? I can only presume to stop forgery or to piss me off altogether which they had already done anyway! So I look on Ticketmaster and see I can pick them up from an outlet as I had done in South Africa but that meant that I would have to sell Dan's in Melbourne which would be a bit of a pain. So I contact Ticketmaster….no reply…. same again no reply. Eventually my 'Australian' address gets me through and Emily god bless her changes them so I can pick up at an outlet with the card I bought them on and some ID.

Better than nothing so I let a friend, Chris Brierley Graham Hughes and John Stubbs know I had two spare going for what I paid for them. It still made me worried about all sorts of stuff prior to pick up like…'But you are a UK passport holder'…'Do you have a utility bill from your Australian address?' On that point I had asked Graham to contact his mate in Sydney to see how I would go about getting the tickets if they had to be posted, he got no reply. I fell back on the fact that Dan had now got the other tickets. He had even sent me a picture and we were meeting him in Adelaide where he had kindly offered to take us to some wineries, lunch and dinner which I insisted would be on us. The easiest thing at this point may have been to give the seated tickets back. But it was the principle involved as I had got them fair and square on a website, after which the ARU and British and Irish Lions PLC perhaps had conspired to try to stop any UK resident from getting tickets other than with the 'official' tours'…

On that subject in May it became clear that the 'official' tours had not sold as many as they would have liked so they were selling them for £409 a throw, this was for bronze tickets! That is $275 Aus for $75 Aus tickets. It is, as I have said many times before legalised touting. In fairness, this price did include entrance to the 'supporters' village and a couple of free drinks! Does that mean if you are not in the 'supporters' village you are clearly not a supporter then?

I will have my say on both the B+I, ARU and Ticketmaster Facebook after the match. What I say will appear in this book later.

In 2009 you may recall Leinster beat Munster in the Heineken Cup semi –final at Croke Park. Alan Quinlan the Munster back rower was cited for gouging Leo Cullen. Quinlan had been picked for the Lions he was banned and missed the tour, Tom Croft replaced him.

The saddest aspect of this is not only does a very good player miss the pinnacle of his career but what happened next. Alan Quinlan got depressed hitting "the bottom of the barrel" and having suicidal thoughts.

The ex-international star has spoken out about how he sank into the depths of depression after that suspension.

"Experiencing depression was a shock and at first I was unwilling to talk about it. It never occurred to me to open up or tell people about my problems."

Thankfully he got through it and now helps others.

On May the 25th 2013, Dylan Hartley a Lions squad member, played for Northampton against Leicester.

Having been warned about talking back to referee Wayne Barnes he was very quickly heard to say 'fucking cheat'. WB was having none of it and sent him off. Hartley was banned for eleven weeks and replaced by Rory Best.

I sincerely hope that Dylan Hartley gets through this massive disappointment without any damage.

On a lighter note, as I have said previously a friend of mine is Graham Hughes a TMO, who I had noticed always refers to people as Whitey, Hughesie etc. I have to say I felt that this was a little over friendly given his independence as a TMO when speaking to a referee. His integrity is in no way in doubt, it was just an observation. This observation was soon put to bed during the aforementioned game when Ben Foden of Northampton went over the line and WB wanted to involve the TMO…….

Hughsie it's Barnsie was the first thing he said…. enough saidsie!

On the 27th of May the majority of the Lions flew out to Hong Kong for the Barbarians game. During the same week I posted my Fantasy Lions teams with the Daily Telegraph and discovered that Sam was out with a knee problem and that O'Connell would Captain what to me was a surprising first up team, which probably made sense in fairness due to most of the team's lack of recent game time. The Baa Baa's had some great players including the great Parisse, Rokocoko and Yashvilli to name a few, the Lions should win but it won't be easy in the heat. Sam's injury concerns me as usually if he has an injury that is him done for a few weeks. Tipuric gets a chance in his place.

THE BARBARIANS – It may be worth here just to give an overview of the second greatest collective team in the world, The Lions of course being the first. I am grateful to the Barbarians website for providing the information.

History of the Barbarians

Many years ago, a group of players were chosen to form an elite team. They had no ground, clubhouse or subscription and membership was by invitation only. In essence they represented a glorious concept brought to life by the vision and enthusiasm of one man, William Percy Carpmael. Inspired by his personal playing experiences with both Blackheath and Cambridge University, his dream was to spread good fellowship amongst all rugby football players. The dream became reality on December 27th 1890 at Friary Field, Hartlepool. There, all things great about the game - flair, courage, spirit and passion - were encapsulated in one great team. A team they called the Barbarians.

Worlds apart

Outstanding talents have followed in their footsteps ever since. Not least the well-remembered Edgar Mobbs. Sadly killed in The Great War, he showed the leadership and spirit required to wear the famous black and white hoops. In his honour, 'The Mobbs Memorial Match' was an annual fixture from 1921 until 2011.

Winning the world over

As a result of many scintillating performances, the Barbarians won respect worldwide and on 31 January 1948 they were invited to play the Australians at Cardiff Arms Park in the final match of the tour. The battle captured the imagination of millions and drew a capacity crowd of 45,000. So successful was the fixture that it became tradition for Australia, New Zealand or South Africa - whichever was touring the UK - to tackle the Barbarians in 'The Final Challenge.' This exciting event took place every three years until the professional era after 1995, games occurred more frequently.

The Modern Game

As the 21st century dawned the Barbarians played South Africa in 2000 and Australia the following year at the Millennium Stadium in Cardiff. Then, in three magical Decembers between 2007 and 2009 (I went to that one), the Barbarians beat South Africa and New Zealand at Twickenham and hosted the first rugby union match at the rebuilt Wembley Stadium, playing Australia in a gala occasion that also celebrated the centenary of the 1908 Olympic Games in London.

Back to 2013

I watched the build up to the Lions first game of the tour and looked forward to the game with great anticipation, and I have to say it was worth the wait. I did think that the Barbarians would be a really difficult test given that they had an un Barbarian like alcohol ban. However the Lions started off really well and kept the momentum going despite the humid and sticky conditions. A number of players played well, especially Mike Phillips, the only real concern I had was the temperament of Owen Farrell during the Schalk Brits incident. Although it was laudable that he was quite happy to dust it up with his long-time team mate. Farrell applauding was not very edifying. I am at this time a little concerned about Sam's fitness as historically if he has an injury it stays around for a while. At this moment in time the 3rd of June (2013) I think that Rob Kearney's participation with a slight hamstring tear is questionable. Amazingly Johnny Wilkinson has been talking about 'having the conversation' with Warren Gatland. My view would be that Johnny has had his opportunity and declined it, therefore if Rob Kearney needs replacing then it should be James Hook for his resilience or Lee Byrne in that order, we will have to wait and see.

Sam is out again against Western Force and BOD takes the captaincy, hope my Fantasy Lions team does better as I have three 'come on boys' will be my test team, '2005' and 'dirt trackers' my other two with a highest league place so far of 5,400 and something not very good really.

My girls got me an early Father's Day present of $60 Aus as I will be away which was very much appreciated and will be wisely spent!

The second game was against a weakened but up for it Western Force side who managed to score two tries, the Lions ran in a number and Leigh Halfpenny never missed a kick. Once again all the Lions put their hands up and no one so far has played poorly. The fly half position however does look like Sexton's. Of concern was the ankle injury to Cian Healey and above that he being cited for an alleged bite. Thankfully he was found not guilty of that but his injury and that of Rob Kearney still cause concern. Alex Corbisero has been drafted in just in case. I personally would have gone for Paul James but there you are. So it is onto Brisbane for perhaps the first big test when captain Sam makes his debut against Quade Cooper and the Reds. On the holiday front the money is ordered and ready for collection, and it is all getting very exciting.

Fantasy Lions wise I managed to jump up to 2,200 and something after the Force game, a very long way to go for me.

The news is now coming thick and fast Cian Healey is out of the tour with ligament damage, and Ryan Grant from Scotland comes in, blimey Paul James is at the back of a very long queue! Sickener for Healey but Vunipola has been playing very well, his Test place is now looking very promising as Gethin Jenkins calf problem has flared up yet again, his further participation is now looking bleak although I would now see him as the Test loosehead with Vunipola coming on as an impact player when legs are getting tired. There is so much rugby on this weekend, the Lions, Wales, England, Scotland, Italy, France, All Blacks and let's not forget the junior World Championship in France, it's a veritable feast, if you have 27 televisions!

As the trip quickly approached, more bad news kept coming from Australia, Gethin Jenkins was on the plane home, Tommy Bowe had broken a finger but was staying with everything crossed. Billy Twelvetrees was being brought in as cover, it gets worse for James Hook, don't think that he will be going now. It hasn't seemed to be a dirty tour so far although the coach of the Waratahs, Michael Chieka, has said before that game that 'anything that moves in a red shirt will get it'. In the 2001 tour this had been correct when Ronan O'Gara was effectively attacked by Duncan McRae. In this renewal it was the Waratahs who were comprehensively beaten 47 v 17, probably the performance of the tour so far.

The Lions skipper Sam Warburton had also laid a wreath in Australia in memory of Bob Seddon who as I have said before died on the first tour, a good touch. Dan had contacted on Facebook and asked that if we had any room could we bring him some Readybrek over. I had just got in but went to the three shops in our village and they didn't have any. Unperturbed an early visit to Tesco completed the task, and it was into the case and under the limit that we went.

I don't know if you do, but I am terrible for checking and checking again when we go on holiday. The evening of the 12th of June was spent checking documents and money as well as suitcase weights. This process was undertaken again the next morning but without any further ado it was into the car and off to Heathrow. Not one for any problems we left five and a half hours before our check in time to make sure of a safe arrival.

Chapter 22
Take off

We had a good trip down to Heathrow and arrived just before midday, so decided to start the tour healthily by partaking of a Kentucky fried chicken. Since I had started my new job, spending much more time on the road I had become a big fan and it beat airport prices anyway. Although I do have to say that the best fried chicken I ever had was in St Mary's, Georgia, USA that was gorgeous and as you would expect in the states, massive, with sides of everything.

We had to wait for a while in the Terminal before booking in as we were early. Why do they call Terminals that, when most people who go through them are actually hoping that they do not drop out of the sky? Terminal, it is so well……...Terminal. Ours was okay and I glimpsed my first Lions shirt, the white one in a young lads' bag as he repacked it. We proceeded through check in, no problem and had our paid for two seats at the back of the Jumbo. I have said on Trip Advisor that BA is getting more and more like an economy airline these days they are after money for everything including double seats and leg room seats. Hey ho it was into Duty Free we go, with Lisa lining up all the 'must have' cosmetics and stuff which is always my treat at the airport, although in fairness she does always offer to pay! The one thing that does confuse me at the airport is the need to have a boarding pass to buy water or chocolate, and I don't mean the seven-foot long Toblerones. It seems a bit daft as you can get it much cheaper outside, although of course you can't bring it in, anyway I get it for fags and booze but it is a bit pointless for a £1.50 bottle of water?

On this trip we had with us a small red plastic Liverpool duck, you may wonder why. Basically in January 2011 a very dear friend of ours at work Chris Barrow contracted swine flu and subsequently died. He was before this a healthy man, it was so sudden and difficult for us at work to take, Bev his wife and family very much more so. Chris was a Liverpool supporter and must have had this as a present at some stage. It was regularly kidnapped while he was alive and held to ransom. Someone came up with a great idea of taking it away and photographing it in various locations. At the time of writing it has been to China, Australia (twice), Thailand and Cambodia, New York, the Cayman Islands and a number of places throughout the UK and long may it continue, Chris is sorely missed.

We had a couple of drinks as we were waiting then it was into the queue to board. A long-time friend of mine Greg works for BA and had said he would see what he could do about an upgrade, as we came to board we heard those great words 'oh you have been upgraded' so it was with great delight that we headed for Premium Economy and a lot more space. Downside was that I did not have my favoured window seat but there you are, can't complain drinks included so I had a few Heinekens as did the duck, and we settled down to watch Gangster Squad, which was good. Once I had drunk enough beer I thought I would have a couple of whiskies, and to save getting up and down thought I would get a couple, so approached the galley and said to one of the cabin staff....'could I have three whiskies please' to which he quite rightly replied 'shall we start with two'...drink responsibly is the motto but I did go back for a couple more. We had taken some crisps on board with us and I was amazed to see how the cabin pressure had doubled the size of the bag, as you can see little things please little minds! I am sure that the crisps had doubled in size as well.

Having had enough and noticed how quickly day had become night and back to day again as we headed towards the sunrise I had a short sleep, and we landed safely in Beijing at 930am on Friday morning. I had expected the checks through customs to be very thorough, but they didn't appear to be and we sailed through into the baggage hall. Our bags for once were quite quick coming through, but I suppose everyone feels that their bags are always last anyway. I can certainly say that ours have never been out first.

So off we toddled with our bags and into arrivals where we were met by our guide 'Mr Peter' with our sign, always a welcome sight when you are in another country. Mr Peter had a driver and en route into the city gave us a potted history of Beijing with its twenty million people and five million cars. It was quite a drive to the Novotel we were staying at but we got there with no issues, booked in and arranged with Mr Peter for our pick up the next day. We got straight into our room and had a few hours' rest. The good thing about our hotel was that it was very near to the city centre. As an example, it took us only ten minutes to walk to the Forbidden City walls:

The Forbidden City was the Chinese imperial palace from the Ming Dynasty to the end of the Qing Dynasty. It is located in the centre of Beijing, China, and now houses the Palace Museum. For almost 500 years, it served as the home of emperors and their households, as well as the ceremonial and political centre of Chinese government.

Built in 1406 to 1420, the complex consists of 980 buildings and covers 720,000 m^2. The palace complex exemplifies traditional Chinese palatial architecture and has influenced cultural and architectural developments in East Asia and elsewhere. The Forbidden City was declared a World Heritage Site in 1987,[2] and is listed *by UNESCO as the largest collection of preserved ancient wooden structures in the world.*

Since 1925, the Forbidden City has been under the charge of the Palace Museum, whose extensive collection of artwork and artefacts were built upon the imperial collections of the Ming and Qing dynasties. Part of the museum's former collection is now located in the National Palace Museum in Taipei. Both museums descend from the same institution, but were split after the Chinese Civil War.

As we walked through the city we overheard a guide saying that the water butts near to some buildings were thought to bring luck if you touched them, they had Lions on them so I touched one twice for two Test wins……see below! It was all down to me after all. The weather I have to say was very hot, about thirty-three degrees, and very humid although there was plenty of water for sale. We came out of the city and then carried on our walk through the modern part where there were many new shopping arcades and on towards Tiananmen Square:

Tiananmen Square is a large city square in the centre of Beijing, China, named after the Tiananmen Gate (Gate of Heavenly Peace) located to its North, separating it from the Forbidden City. Tiananmen Square is the fourth largest square in the world, after Xinghai Square, China, Merdeka Square, Indonesia and Praca dos Girassois in Brazil..

Outside China, the square is best known in recent memory as the focal point of the Tiananmen Square protests of 1989, a pro-democracy movement which ended on 4 June 1989 with the declaration of martial law in Beijing by the government and the death of several hundred or possibly thousands of civilians.

It is a very impressive sight when you get up close and personal and has several pictures of Chairman Mao overlooking proceedings. Sometimes we can remember where we were for historical events. I can remember that when I heard Mao had died on my fourteenth birthday on holiday in Minehead at Butlin's. I heard it on the TV in the TV room where I was watching the Sweeney.... there you are.

Mao Zedong, also transliterated as Mao Tse-tung, commonly referred to as Chairman Mao, was a Chinese communist revolutionary, politician and socio-political theorist. The founding father of the People's Republic of China, he governed the country as Chairman of the Communist Party of China until his death. In this position he converted China into a single-party socialist state, with industry and business being nationalized under state ownership and socialist reforms implemented in all areas of society.

Born the son of a wealthy farmer in Shaoshan, Hunan, Mao adopted a Chinese nationalist and anti-imperialist outlook in early life, particularly influenced by the events of the Xinhai Revolution of 1911 and May Fourth Movement of 1919. In 1922, the Communists agreed to an alliance with the larger Kuomintang (KMT), a nationalist revolutionary party, whom Mao aided in creating a revolutionary peasant army and organising rural land reform. In 1927 the KMT's military leader Generalissimo Chiang Kai-shek broke the alliance and set about on an anti-communist purge; in turn, the CPC formed an army of peasant militia, and the two sides clashed in the Chinese Civil War. Mao was responsible for commanding a part of the CPC's Red Army, and after several setbacks, rose to power in the party by leading the Long March. When the Empire of Japan invaded China in 1937, sparking the Second Sino-Japanese War, Mao agreed to a united front with the KMT. From 1941, both sides fought on the side of the Allies of World War II until Victory over Japan was achieved. The civil war then resumed, in which Mao led the Red Army to victory as Chiang and his supporters fled to Taiwan.

In 1949 Mao proclaimed the foundation of the People's Republic of China, a one-party socialist state controlled by the Communist Party. After solidifying the reunification of China through his Campaign to Suppress Counterrevolutionaries, Mao enacted sweeping land reform, overthrowing the feudal landlords before seizing their large estates and dividing the land into people's communes. He proceeded to lead a nationwide political campaign known as the Great Leap Forward from 1958 through to 1961, designed to modernize and industrialize the country, however agrarian problems worsened by his policies led to widespread famine. In 1966, he initiated the Cultural Revolution, a program to weed out counter-revolutionary elements in Chinese society, which continued until his death.

A deeply controversial figure, Mao is regarded as one of the most important individuals in modern world history.

It was getting towards tea time so we found a nice little beer garden to have a few drinks in. I had learned some very basic Mandarin, but discovered on this trip that it was of no use as it couldn't be understood by anyone. At least I tried is my excuse. In the beer garden, I had an abject failure when trying to find out how strong the beer was! In the end we settled for Yau Jing and it was okay. Eating- wise that night we were quite happy just to eat some buffet and stumbled into the 'Royal' restaurant near our hotel, which looked buffet like. It was more like fine dining, which after a sweaty day we were not really dressed for, but we were in so we stayed in. We had three pork dishes, some beef noodles and a bottle of wine which with the 10% service charge came to Y779 which was about £79………ouch. I also didn't really like how the lady in the restaurant was pretty insistent on standing over us whilst we chose the food, see later but it would appear to be the done thing in some restaurants. The food in fairness was okay.

When watching the Karl Pilkington series an Idiot Abroad I had seen him eat, or being asked to eat 'things' in a night market. That market the Dong Hua Men Night Market was in the same street as our hotel and right outside this restaurant so it had to be done, surely?

There are plenty of stalls and plenty of choice if you like locusts, crickets, centipedes, testicles...yes testicles, I don't know whose. I had a good look around and then plumped for the double small scorpion. I ate the first one with some trepidation, I have to say it was not bad at all and actually tasted like a softer pork scratching, there was plenty of salt on it. I enjoyed the second one too and have the picture to prove it. It was cheap, the market was a really good place to look around and we enjoyed the experience.

We had also tried to find the Da Dong duck restaurant as recommended by none other than Ken Hom, it is quite difficult to find, but we found it; here is an internet address to assist:

http://www.tripadvisor.co.uk/ShowUserReviews-g294212-d1541503-r166389856-Dadong_Roast_Duck_Restaurant_Jinbao_Place-Beijing.html

That could now wait until tomorrow, it had been a long old day so we toddled off to bed very pleased with what we had achieved.

As always that night's sleep was easily found and we both slept very well. The next day was again very warm, and we were ready for Mr Peter when he arrived at the hotel. Our first stop was in the Hutongs. These are basically a series of narrow streets or alleys where houses are situated in small court yards. They are mostly associated with northern China and most prominently Beijing. We were escorted through the streets by a guide on foot and on a rickshaw which was far safer than our experience in India. A lot of the houses had red as the colour of the doors, we were told this was for luck. There were also lions on a lot of them this was to ward off evil spirits. We also noticed that a lot of cars had covers placed next to their tyres, intrigued by this we asked the guide why. It was, he said, to stop the dogs weeing on the tyres. I thought it would be something completely different. The whole place was very tidy, an equivalent over here I suppose, would be our beloved terraced streets although we were invited into one residence and they had a bit more room. The home being served by several rooms off a central courtyard. I say invited in, what I meant to say was some of our tour money had gone to the lady whose house it was to let her mother us for ten minutes. Or even worse the family had been kicked out whilst the tourists moved in, perhaps I am being a little harsh. Our tour ended on the wall by the water where the guide reminded us that although it was very humid, in the winter the temperature could drop to minus twenty, and all the water would be frozen for weeks.

Our next stop was the Great Wall of China at Mutianyu, en route Mr Peter explained to me that Peking had become Beijing because the former was its Cantonese name, the latter the mandarin version. This had all come about in 1980.

Mutianyu is a section of the Great Wall of China located in Huairou County 70 km northeast of central Beijing. The Mutianyu section of the Great Wall is connected with Jiankou in the west and Lianhuachi in the east. As one of the best-preserved parts of the Great Wall, the Mutianyu section of the Great Wall used to serve as the northern barrier defending the capital and the imperial tombs.

First built in the mid-6th century during the Northern Qi, Mutianyu Great Wall is older than the Badaling section of the Great Wall. In the Ming dynasty, under the supervision of General Xu Da, construction of the present wall began on the foundation of the wall of Northern Qi. In 1404, a pass was built in the wall. In 1569, the Mutianyu Great Wall was rebuilt and till today most parts of it are well preserved. The Mutianyu Great Wall has the largest construction scale and best quality among all sections of Great Wall.

Built mainly with granite, the wall is 7–8.5 metres high and the top is 4–5 metres wide. Compared with other sections of Great Wall, Mutianyu Great Wall possesses unique characteristics in its construction.

- *Watchtowers are densely placed along this section of the Great Wall - 22 watchtowers on this 2,250-metre-long stretch.*
- *Both the outer and inner parapets are crenelated with merlons, so that shots could be fired at the enemy on both sides - a feature very rare on other parts of the Great Wall.*
- *The Mutianyu Pass consists of 3 watchtowers, one big in the centre and two smaller on both sides. Standing on the same terrace, the three watchtowers are connected to each other inside and compose a rarely seen structure among all sections of Great Wall.*

Besides, this section of Great Wall is surrounded by woodland and streams. The forest-coverage rate is over 90 percent.

There are three methods of ascent and four methods of descent to choose from. Besides utilising 4000+ steps, visitors may also choose between a two-rider chairlift or four-rider gondola up from the foothills to the level of the wall, which runs along the ridges above. These lifts may also be used to descend. Another feature of the wall at Mutianyu is an alternate method of descent by single-rider personal wheeled toboggan. This allows single riders to descend from the wall to the valley on a winding metal track.

We took the chair lift, Mr Peter didn't look too happy as we rode up, I wasn't too keen on it, neither was

Lisa but it was okay. The wall itself is extremely impressive. We walked along about half a mile of it, on any other day we may have gone further but it was very humid. Definitely one off the list.

On our return from the wall we passed the usual tourist shops and I was taken to buy our usual piece of tourist tat for the bathroom, but it was too pricey here! We stopped off for lunch which was plentiful and very nice Chinese fayre. A drop at the hotel left us open to our own devices so I went out to find and book Da Dong. I did find an Irish pub on the way Molly Malones which had a dart board as well. After a quick change, we went for a wander and found a 'two for one' bar at the Park Plaza in Jiantao Street. From here we went to our booking at Da Dong. The restaurant inside was contemporary with the centre piece being where the ducks are prepared. I have to say the menu was probably the most complicated in history and again we had to suffer someone standing over us as we chose. I understand this is to help, but if you are not used to it, it becomes annoying. We ordered a duck, obviously and I went for Crucian Carp which was blackened and served cold, I enjoyed it, Lisa not so the Scampi. But the Duck was excellent. I can imagine that there would be some back-street restaurant where it would be better but Ken hadn't shown me that. Back to the hotel it was and a doze off whilst watching Madmen in mandarin!

The next day saw us being picked up for the journey to the airport and flight to Xi'an. No problems at the airport although I was a little concerned that Aircraft Investigation was being shown on the TV! I did manage to pick up some Lions news which was that Shane Williams had been drafted in to play as had Brad Barritt and Christian Wade. There was a lot of comment about Shane coming in, that others deserved a chance. The reality was that he was on his way into Australia anyway and had been playing recently in Japan. It didn't work out in the end but I thought that it was not a bad idea really.

Our flight was very bumpy and we were glad that it was only two hours. We were met on time by our new guide Miss Susan. She gave us a great potted history of the area and the royal families as we drove into the walled city.

Xi'an is the capital of Shaanxi Province, and a sub-provincial city in China. One of the oldest cities in China, with more than 3,100 years of history, the city was known as Chang'an before the Ming Dynasty. Xi'an is one of the Four Great Ancient Capitals of China, having held the position under several of the most important dynasties in Chinese history, including Zhou, Qin (Chin), Han, Sui, and Tang (Tongue). Xi'an is the starting point of the Silk Road and home to the Terracotta Army of Emperor Qin Shi Huang.

She told us about Eunuchs and Concubines in the Imperial court. I have to say I have always got a little confused about what this means. Generally, a Eunuch was a man who had been castrated or is celibate. A Concubine is a woman who lives with a man, but is not married to him and is considered at a lower level than his wife/wives.

We drove over the Yellow river where I said to Miss Susan 'Is this the Yangtze' to be met quite firmly with 'No that is much further north!' For some reason I had always confused the two, probably after listening to the Monty Python sketch as a boy; did it go 'O Yangtse beautiful Yangtse full of carp and trout and perch and bream' find out for yourself. Here it is…...
.

http://www.youtube.com/watch?
v=bqymo3K8Cxg

Our hotel was very nice a Mercure, although it was set in a compound, there were bars but we wanted to experience a bit of the real China. Our receptionist when I asked where the locals would go directed us to the De Fu Xiang area which was basically near to the northern old city walls. Although it was still around thirty degrees we decided having been given a map that we would walk. It was north approximately two miles across the city, we got the buzz of the place and were also able to see both the Bell and Drum towers in daylight and at night, very impressive. Armed with De Fu Xiang written in English and Mandarin by the receptionist we found the area with the help of a local Police officer, who saw the mandarin and delightedly pointed the way. We were proper hot by the time we reached here and saw a good few restaurants with a street just off that had bars. We knew Tsing Tao was a beer so had a few cold ones of that as we watched the world go by. You know those 'finds' when you are on holiday, well here was one of them, quality.

So it was off to find somewhere to eat, and herein was a slight problem, the first restaurant we went into saw my mandarin fail dismally and I couldn't even describe getting a drink of water despite pointing at a glass of water and doing all the mimicking that I could. Eventually we were led to where the food was, which we picked up was a system where you picked it and they cooked it. Anyway, having picked some ribs at twenty-eight yuan we were shown that we had to have the forty eight yuan version. Probably because there were none of the other ones left. However as I, as well as the waitress, was now completely frustrated I called a halt to proceedings and we left the premises. Probably all very entertaining for those who were eating.

We crossed the road and found a place called, if I am correct from the business card, Ding Ding Xiang Can Yin. In here they had menus…. but with pictures on……. result. The staff were absolutely charming…and the food wow, we went to town and had deep fried mushrooms, a chilli pie, we only wanted one piece but the lot came, and we also had ribs in a type of stew. A couple of beers and complimentary tea all washed it down, and as the only non-locals in there we provided the entertainment for everyone. The bill was one hundred and fifty-nine yuan which translates to about sixteen pounds I rounded up the bill to two hundred yuan but the lady who looked after this refused. When I asked Miss Susan why this was she told me that in local areas tipping wasn't expected in fact they would wonder why you would pay them extra for doing a job that they were being paid to do.

Wish that happened in some other places, America for an example. Generally as Brits we are ten percenters if that. In Fort Walton in Florida once we had some lovely service from a lady and I tipped ten per cent, although the receipt had notes about tipping up to forty per cent depending on the service. After I reviewed the place on trip advisor I had a message from a waitress in America deriding me saying this was how they made their money. I think that she calmed down when I told her this wasn't our way and it was up to her employer, not me, to make sure that she was paid a living wage not mine.

Back to Xi'an and we had a nice walk home and loved seeing the locals in one park happily line dancing the night away.

The next day saw us being picked up by Miss Susan quite early. It was very hot, about thirty-five degrees, so hot that Miss Susan was moaning about the heat and was using an umbrella to keep in the shade. Despite this she was an excellent guide.

Our first stop was the Wild Goose Pagoda:

The original pagoda was built during the reign of Emperor Gaozong of Tang then standing at a height of 177 ft. However, this construction of rammed earth with a stone exterior facade eventually collapsed five decades later. The ruling Empress Wu Zetian had the pagoda rebuilt and added five new stories by the year 704; in 1556 an earthquake badly damaged the pagoda and reduced it by three stories, to its current height of seven stories. The entire structure leans very perceptibly to the west.

We had visited some Buddhist sites in India the previous year, being a Roman Catholic, if not practicing I have some views on the subject of the afterlife. My belief is that our body is just a vessel that carries our soul, that part that is us. The part that you feel the world around you. I think that when your day comes it is just this vessel that dies. However I think that your soul lives on and we are effectively born again. I think that is why some people have those experiences which would suggest that they have been here before. This is why we get *déjà-vu*? I also think that you can be born again into a time that has passed, a time now or a time in the future. Some physicists theoretically would support this as parallel universe. In that there are universes going on alongside our own. There is also an old theory of 'box time' which means that what happened to you last Wednesday is still going on in another place. This can give comfort when you have lost loved ones, in that if you remember a nice time with them, that day is still going on in another place and they are experiencing it. The positive for us, although we can't join them we have the memory of that day. So my views are a little Buddhist, a little RC and a little theoretical Physics. There are other similarities between Buddhism and Catholicism. Buddha's mother before she became pregnant was visited by a white elephant, she then became pregnant, the Virgin Mary was visited by the Angel Gabriel. Food for thought.

On the way out of the temple I wrote down my golf ball mark and asked Miss Susan if she knew what it meant? She said that she did and that it was the Chinese symbol for Believe. I was glad because that is what I thought it was! It is the symbol below on the right I put it on my golf balls during a bad playing spell, it helped…. a little.

相信

BELIEVE

FREETATTOODESIGNS.ORG

Back to the main reason for our being in Xi'an, the Terracotta Army. Miss Susan was full of information and told us that we may see the farmer who had found the army in 1974. I really didn't understand what she meant and imagined that we would pass the farmer at a stall of something. Anyway, once we got to the entrance before we knew it we were in a shop and in front of us, we were told was the said farmer. He smiled we smiled, we had a photo with him and in a flourish, I had a DVD, postcards and a book signed in front of me by the farmer in my hand and it was thirty-five quid please. I am usually very good at avoiding this nonsense but this was so slick I was done for and tapping my PIN in before you could say terracotta. At least the brush used to sign was in our bag, or so I thought, I saw it go in, but didn't see it coming out! When we checked later it wasn't, done like a kipper!

Even worse I said to Lisa later how did we know he was the actual farmer? Fact was we didn't in fact I wondered out loud whether they had all been in the pub on the night before:

'who is going to be the farmer tomorrow????'

My turn!

This theory was enhanced when some months later we watched 'More secrets of the terracotta army' on Channel 4. The farmer on that programme was definitely not the farmer we had seen. As I said, done like a kipper!

The Army was discovered on 29 March 1974 to the east of Xi'an in Shaanxi province by a group of farmers when they were digging a water well. For centuries, there had been occasional reports of pieces of terracotta figures and fragments of the Qin necropolis – roofing tiles, bricks, and chunks of masonry – having been dug up in the area. This most recent discovery prompted Chinese archaeologists to investigate, and they unearthed the largest pottery figurine group ever found in China.

In addition to the warriors, an entire man-made necropolis for the Emperor has also been found around the first Emperor's tomb mound. The tomb mound is located at the foot of Mount Li as an earthen pyramid,[7] and Qin Shi Huangdi's necropolis complex was constructed as a microcosm of his imperial palace or compound. It consists of several offices, halls, stables and other structures placed around the tomb mound which is surrounded by two solidly built rammed earth walls with gateway entrances.

According to historian Sima Qian work on this mausoleum began in 246 BC soon after Emperor Qin ascended the throne (then aged 13), and the full construction later involved 700,000 workers. Sima wrote that the First Emperor was buried with palaces, towers, officials, valuable artefacts and wonderful objects. According to this account, there were 100 rivers simulated with flowing mercury, and above them the ceiling was decorated with heavenly bodies below which were the features of the land. It was even said that the tomb had night and day.

Recent scientific work at the site has found high levels of mercury in the soil of the tomb mound, giving some credence to Sima Qian's account of the emperor's tomb.

The tomb remains unopened, one possible reason may be concerns about the preservation of valuable artefacts once the tomb is opened. For example, after their excavation, the painted surface present on some figures of the terracotta army began to flake and fade.

Wouldn't it be something if they opened it and was as Sima said the biggest wonder ever, I wonder why they can't send probes just to have a little look. Maybe not in my time but sometime, and given the Chinese need for raw materials maybe sooner rather than later! One of the things I did notice as we walked around the site the practice of hocking…you know getting ready to spit a horrendously popular thing to do in China as it is in India; it's disgusting, sorry. Another thing that I saw and asked Miss Susan about was a lot of Chinese men with their tee shirts rolled up exposing their midriff. This was apparently to keep them cool as they are not allowed to take the top completely off. I wish someone would do that over here when our lot are sweating about in the towns and cities on sometimes not even warm days. Nevertheless, we had enjoyed the army and the meal that was provided as part of the deal. Although why the cruise ship party were eating I do not know?

Have you ever been on a cruise, for me the worst part is the food, why does it need to be available twenty-four seven? I know you can say no but the fact is that you don't do you? You just have to pick away and instead of having one thing for lunch have about five, and then eat in the afternoon when you don't need it. It goes on and on. As they always do the Americans in the party loudly pointed out to everyone what was going on in the kitchen and where the noodles were being made, we all knew we could see what was happening. On one cruise, we did there was an art auction, which would have been fine but the auctioneer insisted on making it loud…….and louder assisted by his country people. He even said at one stage that he would get the Brits going as loud, he didn't we refused en bloc and left the noise in droves. Why do a lot of Americans have to be so loud? Is it a national insecurity or am I being unfair? There are a lot of very nice Americans in fairness.

I am not sure about you but when I see something famous I like to get the wow factor. The Saturn five rocket at Cape Canaveral had it, the Pyramids had it……and so did the Terracotta Army, they have to be seen to be believed it really is quite amazing. I would have loved to have been able to see them two thousand years ago, when they were in their pomp. Miss Susan told us that the Emperor's original idea had been to have the real army in his tomb alive! He was only dissuaded when his advisors pointed out that there would be no one to protect them when he died if he did. I did ask Miss Susan why the Army had not been found before, she said that they probably had but the people would have been scared and thought that to dig them up would release evil spirits. TMO Graham Hughes thinks that it's all a hoax and effectively the Chinese 'Disneyland'. I think that it is what it is.

Back to the hotel we went and I managed to get some news on the Lions, Jamie Roberts was now a doubt as was George North, I felt that we would still have a good team, but injuries were worrying. On the subject of sport Justin Rose had won the US Open, a great result.

We decided to go back to the same restaurant and area as we had on the first night, this time we cut back a little on the food but it was still plenty, very nice and cheap again. There was a slight problem when we got back to the hotel. There was a bloke behind the reception who either thought that he was above doing nights, or above me or above everyone else his attitude was pants:

'What time is breakfast please?'
'Seventy-five yuan'
'No what times are breakfast?'
'Six to ten thirty'
'Thank you'
'Where is the pool please?'
'Over there' points to his left.
'Where is over there? Somewhere in Xi'an or the East wing of the hotel?'
'East wing of the hotel'
'Can I have some ice please'
'You want ice?'
'Yes please, not a lot just a glassful'
'What is your room number?'
'Just give me a glass of ice'
'Room number'

I gave it to him and about five minutes later a lady arrived with a bucketful. The swimming pool and spa bit were, however, very nice. Breakfast was okay as well, I wasted most of the ice.

Next day we had quite a leisurely morning, and were picked up by Miss Susan for the drive to the airport. No problems there although we did have some problems getting rid of all of the Yuan. The water was okay, but what I thought were crisps were some horrible rice cakes which we never did eat, and a bit of chocolate which we did. The flight to Hong Kong was uneventful but I did note that on both our short flights in China meals and drinks had been complimentary, they won't be for long.

I pride myself on being a 'systems thinker' there are many books, journals and articles about this topic but in lay persons' terms it is all about looking at a process and stripping out the waste. Imagine yourself at the left-hand bottom corner of a box, many people would walk along two sides to get to the top right hand corner, I find it easier if you can to walk straight across the box.

With that now firmly in your thoughts imagine the scene at Hong Kong airport once we had cleared the carousal. You know the feeling you are tired you want to get to your hotel and your 'package' includes transport to said hotel. First we had to find our transfer people, we did quite quickly as their dress had been described to us in the holiday documents. Once we had found this nice gentleman in a very catching green jacket, he smiled and directed us to a desk. When we got there the lady smiled and directed us to some seats, where we sat for around twenty minutes getting us very frustrated and we were not the only ones. We had been off the aircraft for around forty minutes by this time. The next part of the process was that a man came and asked us to follow him, which we all did, he took us to a lift and then down some floors and out into a garage type place...and told us to wait there, he then walked off. We stayed there for about another ten minutes, then another man came and took us further on in our adventure to some more seats, but this was better they were near to some coaches. After about another ten minutes another man came and pointed us to our coach after asking for our hotel name. I know that these things need managing but all those who were at the first seats got on the same coach. So the systems thinker in me wondered, aloud.........on several occasions why there could not have been a sign saying 'make your way to the coach park' in the first place. It would have been far easier and less stressful. I do very much appreciate it would not have created as many jobs, if that was the case they should have said and I would have shut up and hung around aimlessly for ages.

Onto the coach we went and into the very bright lights of the Hong Kong skyline. It was a lot bigger than I thought and the trip, although enjoyable took a bit longer than expected, but thankfully we were the first drop at the Metro park Causeway. Booking in was very good and I thought that our room 2005, that being a Lions year was an omen. I would agree it being a losing year it could have been a bad omen, but I decided to follow it anyway, and I have followed a few omens in the past! Believe me.

It was now getting on a little bit, we had eaten on the plane, as well as the rubbish we had got from the airport so we went straight out, and into the first bar we saw enticed by the 'happy hour' sign. Well if this was happy hour prices in Hong Kong I would have been gutted if I was a resident. Our Carlsberg cost £3.73 each not so happy then we had one each and walked down the hill a bit. Actually, this was a good idea as it was less touristy and very authentic, so we dropped into a café and had a few Asashi at about £1.30, should have come here first, we also tried a long-legged crab appetiser which was very good. We then went back to the hotel, Lisa for a sleep and me to go to the bar and see if I could catch the Lions result. I just about caught the happy hour in the hotel, and the Lions result, despite Shane playing again they had lost narrowly to the Brumbies, the first loss on tour.

The first loss for me always seems to hit the hardest. But it was a scratch team up against a strong super 15 side, don't panic. I did write in my notes the team I now thought would start the first test given the injury news at that time:

Vunipola (**Corbisiero**), Hibbard (**Youngs T.**), Jones A., O'Connell, Jones A.W, Croft, Warburton, Heaslip, Phillips, Sexton, Maitland (**North**), Tuilagi (**Davies**), O'Driscoll, Cuthbert, Halfpenny

Not a bad shout really, although given John Davies's form he should have been in my team, scratched out in the lounge in Hong Kong.

The next day we decided to have a good walk around the part of Hong Kong we were in…….it was very hot but nevertheless we managed to get up to the Hong Kong stadium and get a picture of Chris's duck in situ. Down in the main shopping area my currency converter went on the blink when I almost bought two Paul and Le Shark polo shirts. They were priced at $1200 Hong Kong dollars and I thought that $100 equated to £1 so thought that I was on a winner until the last minute when I realised that the exchange rate was actually £1 to $13, a close call so I didn't buy them from the 'bargain' section. Due to the heat we had a quick snack from a market, a lot of water then went back to the hotel for a swim. The hotel had a great pool which was on the roof top and gave us some great views across the harbours. The water was nice as well so the duck also went for a swim. The only thing that spoiled the tranquillity was a loud group of Russian women having a shouting conversation which truncated our quiet time on the roof. Never mind onwards and upwards there were other things to do, like go to the Jumbo restaurant for some drinks and tea. I had been told about the floating Jumbo restaurants many years before when I was in the Royal Navy. It had always been on my mind so now was a chance to do it. We decided to use the public transport system, and for this I would strongly advise the use of an Octopus card. The initial outlay seems quite high but remember that most of it is taken up by a deposit that you will get back at the end of the day. This had fooled us when we used it for our first underground trip but the information booth staff soon pointed out our error. We used it for the rest of the day on the bus and underground and it was excellent value.

After an underground trip and two buses followed by a quick ferry trip we found ourselves at the Jumbo floating restaurant where we passed a couple of hours on one of the balconies shooting the breeze and having a drink. We also ate here, along with another cruise ship full of Americans who really didn't need the food before dinner back on the ship! We had sweet and sour pork, crispy chicken and a deep-fried seafood selection which was all very nice. We then popped back on the ferry to get a bus to take us to the underground, to cross the water for the Hong Kong skyline light show. On the bus we passed the Happy Valley racetrack which looked very good in the dusky light. There were loads of people going to the light show but I do have to say that I thought that some of the signage to the area and certainly signage for the station coming back was not very good at all. As for the light show I am afraid we thought that it's write up was better than the actual show a bit disappointing if we were honest, but never mind we got back to the hotel for the happy hour.

Chapter 23
Return to Oz

We were moving on again and resplendent in one of my Lions tops we were up early to wait for the bus, which as is the norm had a number of other stops before we headed for the airport. On the last stop we waited, and we waited and waited some more for the lone, late American to eventually get on the bus. Of course whilst not apologising to anyone. This happens too often for me, okay some people can't help it but most think that the world is waiting for them. I wasn't and if I could have done would have driven off without this ignorant individual or Mr Todd who had been staying at the Marriott as I will name him. Lateness is a malaise that people put up with for no apparent reason at all.

There were no problems at the airport and it was here that I saw one of our first Lions touring parties. Ian McGeechan says in 1997 when talking to the squad that in future years they may see each other across the road, when there would be no need to say anything a nod would suffice to acknowledge their part in something extraordinary. I think that it is the same with the supporters, you all feel part of something different. This was very much the case here as we passed the 'Pompey Boys' walking towards security I looked across at one of their group and there was a smile, and a wink in acknowledgement that we were on the way to something special, something very different.

Due to Quantas jumping in with Emirates we had to get to Perth via a stopover in Singapore. This also meant that the leg room seats that we had paid for were not now available on this leg of the flight. This turned out not to be a problem as we were subsequently refunded on our return home. The three-and-a-half-hour flight to Singapore was not very pleasant it was quite bumpy and we landed in what could only be called smog, due to deliberate forest fires in Indonesia. The visibility was really quite poor. We didn't have long to wait until our Perth flight for which we now had some leg room seats.

The flight to Perth started well there was some Australian real ale available to drink and Zero Dark Thirty available on the movies. Sadly, we also found out that James Gandolfini, the actor had died suddenly in Italy. That was a real shame I was a big fan of the Sopranos so it was sad to see him go relatively young. We also discovered that one of the cabin crew was originally from the UK. Here name was Carol Dowson, we got chatting because, as seemed to be the case on this trip the flight experienced some rough weather. In this case a huge electrical storm which we had to fly around. The captain had given the command that we all don't like 'All passengers and crew return to your seats and put on your seat belts'. On this occasion it gave us the opportunity to speak with Carol who had gone to Australia when she was twenty-one and had stayed. She was originally from Ruislip and her husband not too far from us, Bredbury. The aforementioned storm was off to our left and was spectacular to say the least, it was lighting up the whole sky and must have been hundreds of miles across, because it took us half an hour to get past it. The clouds were alight, sheet lightening like I have never seen, and overall a vicious violent sky, thank god for radar! It was with relief that Carol was allowed up to carry on with her work and we could all relax and get back to the real ale which was James Squire and not too bad.

We arrived in Perth after midnight and were picked up and taken to our hotel the Four Points. We breezed through check in and sank into our bed after a long day. Shame we were in room 401, it was so noisy so we didn't sleep a great deal. When we got up we went to reception and they changed our room no problem. The reason for the noise was that we were right next to the lift shaft, bad design not planning. Due to the lack of sleep we were up early and I went into town to pick up the tickets, still convinced that somehow, I would be thwarted. Doogues is a chain of shops and it was here, without any ado I picked up the tickets which were printed off for me on production of my receipt. I was immensely relieved we had what we came for. But Dan also had two for us so we needed to sell two, I didn't think that this would be a problem. I later posted the below on the Ticketmaster Facebook page after the cancellation of a concert by 'Frank';

Sorry about Frank hope he gets well. Anyway last year I joined Ticketmaster Australia with the hope of getting Lions tickets my registration although with a UK address was never challenged. I was also allowed to highlight my venue and event which was the 2nd test in Melbourne. I received constant reminders of this. Imagine my horror when I was advised by Ticketmaster that basically anyone with a UK address couldn't have tickets? See above for registration and also is that actually legal? Anyway, I continued on my odyssey and in hope rather than anything else went for tickets when they opened and I actually got two GOLD tickets......brilliant until I get an e-mail saying I must have an Australian address?? Is that legal?.... I got one, then we could not print them off?? However, after many sleepless nights I got the tickets that I had lawfully purchased. Some of the things that went on meant that many like me were not really given a 'fair go' and some of it was clearly 'un-Australian'. As a reminder, the British and Irish Lions sell tickets to us with the proviso we either pay way over the price or we buy their plane tickets locations and hotels and go on holiday when they want us to. Clearly unfair but not helped by the above circumstances.

The plan for the rest of the day was to have a look around Perth, and then go into Fremantle for some drinks and something to eat. We walked up to Kings Park.

The park is located on the western edge of the central business district, it has a mixture of grassed parkland, botanical gardens and natural bushland on Mount Eliza with two thirds of the grounds conserved as native bushland. There are panoramic views of the Swan River and Darling Range, it is home to over 300 native plant varieties and 80 bird species. It overlooks the city as well as Perth Water and Melville Water on the Swan River.

It is one of the largest inner city parks in the world and the most popular visitor destination in Western Australia, being visited by over five million people each year. The park is larger than New York's Central Park.

The streets are tree lined with individual plaques dedicated by family members to Western Australian service men and women who died in World War I and World War II.

I paid particular attention to the memorial to the Light Horsemen, having seen a film of the same name some years before. The charge scene was fantastic.

The Australian Light Horse were mounted troops who served in the Second Boer War and World War I that combined characteristics of both cavalry and mounted infantry. This was the outcome of doctrinal debate in military circles in Australia in the late 19th century concerning the future of mounted troops. The example of the Franco-Prussian War illustrated that the battlefield had become dominated by massed land armies supported by artillery. For Australia, the reality was vast spaces with sparse populations making it difficult to consider anything that remotely looked like the European model. The 1890s were wracked by drought and depression ensuring that none of the states were able to afford anything but the most token of armies supported by a large contingent of volunteers.

The Second Boer War provided the short-term answer. While Australian forces fought against the Boers in South Africa, the Boer methodology of conducting war was considered to be the answer for Australian defence. Volunteer Light Horse Regiments were established around Australia supported by the Rifle Club movement which provided semi trained reinforcements for the various formations. Should these formations be called upon to defend Australia, the local commander was charged with maintaining resistance through the use of the Commando formation which envisaged a large-scale guerrilla war. The prospect of an endless and strength sapping guerrilla war was the key deterrent factor which relied heavily upon mobile soldiers. The mounted infantry remained the key to the Australian defence posture until the Kitchener Report of 1910 which envisaged formations that could be slotted directly into an Imperial expeditionary force. The plan envisaged two mounted divisions.

Light horse were like mounted infantry in that they usually fought dismounted, using their horses as transport to the battlefield and as a means of swift disengagement when retreating or retiring. A famous exception to this rule though was the charge of the 4th and 12th Light Horse Regiments at Beersheba on 31 October 1917. In 1918 some light horse regiments were equipped with sabres, enabling them to fight in a conventional cavalry role in the advance on Damascus. However, unlike mounted infantry, the light horse also performed certain roles, such as scouting and screening, while mounted.

I found that film inspiring and given Australia's relatively small population at the time of the First World War, I was amazed at how many Australian names are etched onto the Menin Gate at Ypres. Where those dead but not forgotten are remembered every night. Rightly so.

The walk was nice it was a sunny day and we were up there for a couple of hours before walking down to the train station. Perth is not that big a city really, so fairly easy to walk around even if it is a little hilly in places.

We had decided on a visit to Fremantle after having heard many years ago about a wind the 'Freemantle Doctor' which was regularly referred to during test match coverage from the WACA. I had also discovered that there was a real ale microbrewery to be found 'Little Creatures' and there were some fish and chip restaurants to be had, so it would make a nice little trip. We saw a seat in the station that was used by Lenny Sexton, 1911 – 1979, apparently, a local legend who spent his days here telling people which trains they could catch, he was known, or had been known as the 'Human Timetable'. Our train came soon enough and with our $8Aus return tickets we were off through the suburbs and down the coast to Perth.

The journey itself was uneventful and we found the walk around Fremantle pretty easy, it was quite bohemian in places, and we particularly enjoyed the indoor market which was very independent. Our journey uncovered some interesting facts like the late Bon Scott ex of AC/DC had lived for a time in Freemantle after moving over from Scotland via Melbourne. We also discovered a Victoria Cross recipient;

Air Commodore Sir Hughie Idwal Edwards VC, KCMG, CB, DSO, OBE, DFC (1 August 1914 – 5 August 1982) was a senior officer in the Royal Air Force, Governor of Western Australia, and an Australian recipient of the Victoria Cross, the highest decoration for gallantry "in the face of the enemy" that can be awarded to members of the British and Commonwealth armed forces. Serving as a bomber pilot in the Royal Air Force, Edwards was decorated with the Victoria Cross in 1941 for his efforts in leading a bombing raid against the port of Bremen, one of the most heavily-defended towns in Germany. He became the most highly-decorated Australian serviceman of the Second World War.

Born in Fremantle, Western Australia, Edwards joined the Royal Australian Air Force in 1935, and a year later was granted a short service commission with the Royal Air Force. Serving with the RAF throughout the Second World War, he gained a permanent commission and continued his career in the RAF after the war; he retired in 1963 with the rank of air commodore. Returning to Australia, he was made Governor of Western Australia in 1974.

Our walk took us to the Fremantle Oval and eventually we ended up at the seafront, it was a lovely sunny afternoon and there was a breeze, so I am having that as the 'Doctor'. After a brief lie down we headed into 'Little Creatures' microbrewery which was pretty busy. Here we discovered the exorbitant cost of Australian beer it was ridiculous really over £5 for a pint, I was to learn that the recession had not hit Australia so wages were high as were the prices. I knew it was coming but it still hurts when it arrives! Despite this we spent a nice couple of hours there. We then moved on to the 'best fish and chips' at Cicerello's. Well the fish was certainly up there, the type that tastes as if it has just come out of the sea very nice, but what no mushy peas, no curry sauce, sorry well behind some of the chip shops in Blighty in that respect. Never mind it was fine and our little trip had been very good, Fremantle is well worth a visit. The train was no problem going back and it was only a short walk back to the hotel and had a night cap that was somewhat spoilt by some Brits in the bar, a couple of those idiots who frequent bars and public transport. You know the sort shouting about large amounts of money they have or are going to be earning or spending. Usually referring to thousands as K, usually talking bollocks. I will move on we did and had a good night's sleep, we had walked miles.

The next morning at breakfast there was a British couple sat down, why the lady needed to wear sunglasses, in a dark breakfast room while she did I don't know. I wasn't about to point this out to her partner/husband he looked the part. Had clearly had several broken noses and I have never seen anyone eat so much at breakfast. Left them to it, maybe he liked the glasses. The centre of Perth has a lot of eighteen hundred style buildings which give it a certain character, the centre is mainly in a grid so that gave us the opportunity to use that to cover most of it. So, we walked up and down St Georges Terrace, Hay Street and the main drag Murray Street and came across a Woolworths and what was to become one of our favourites…. a pie shop. Didn't really know that the Aussies were into pies but they were so we joined in with gusto almost everywhere. As we walked we also found a prospective viewing bar for the rugby, it was the day of the first Test, Durty Nelly where $7.50 pints of Guinness were on offer, about £3.80 believe me that was a bargain and also $18

T bones which would do very nicely after the match. It was $5.50 for a half of Heineken, about £3.00. All set we now made for the major sporting attraction in Perth known to all cricket devotees simply as the WACA, short for Western Australian Cricket Association.

"Home" of cricket in Western Australia since the early 1890s, the first Test match played at the ground was in 1970. The WACA is the home ground of Western Australia's first-class cricket team, the Western Warriors and the local Big Bash League franchise, the Perth Scorchers. The women's cricket team known as the Western Fury plays in the Women's National Cricket League.

The pitch at the WACA is regarded as one of the quickest and bounciest in the world, the outfield is also exceptionally fast. These characteristics, in combination with the afternoon sea-breezes which regularly pass the ground (the Fremantle Doctor), have historically made the ground an attractive place for pace and swing bowlers. The ground has seen some very fast scoring – as at December 2012, four of the seven fastest Test centuries had been scored at the WACA.

Throughout its history, the ground has also been used for a range of other sports, including athletics carnivals, Australian rules football, baseball, soccer, rugby league, rugby union, and international rules football. However, recent years have seen most of these activities relocated to other venues. It has also been used for major rock concerts.

It is a huge ground and took some walking around, but we had plenty of time, and even time for a slight snooze back at the hotel before getting kitted for the Lions. I chose the New Zealand 2005 shirt, it had a lucky factor of won one (watching the 3rd Test on TV in 2009) and lost one (being at the 2nd Test in 2009). Hopefully this would be the change. Quick drink in the hotel bar and it was off to Durty Nelly's in plenty of time to get a good seat and soak up the atmosphere. There were plenty of gold shirts in the bar, but a good few red ones as well. I love being at live events, but if you can't the pub is a good alternative.

We were all set, as with most people I get animated watching sport and this can be compounded in the pub because there is more room. I was once told quietly to 'sit down' when under the TV celebrating Scott William's try at Twickenham in 2012, the same was to happen here. I thought that the Lions had started off pretty well but it was pretty even-steven in that first half although Israel Folau was and would be causing us problems. Then the Australians kicked the ball to Giant George in space. There is nothing more beautiful for me than seeing a great rugby back in space, and that would be the case here. George picked it up about seventy metres out and he was off, picking up speed and evading tackles as he went, as he crossed the half way line I was out of my seat 'come on Georgy' in a low voice. He breezed towards the Australian twenty-two, the TV was now getting closer 'go George come on', Genia frantically tried to cover across, we held our breath, George breezed past and over the line. I was now under the TV screaming 'get in get in, come on boys' pure elation, the Lions in the pub were also going mad, absolute brilliance. However, things did not push on from there and it really became nip and tuck, despite another great try from Alex Cuthbert as we went deep into the second half. My animation was becoming worse as the final whistle moved closer. It was around this stage that a man who had been sitting to our left came over to me. He said that he had come in to watch the rugby, but had ended up watching me, he said he had never seen anyone so passionate about a game of rugby. I was pretty pleased with that I have to say. It turned out he was cabin crew for Quantas. Back to the rugby, James O'Connor's kicking had not been the best and Beale came on to replace him and was kicking well, he too offered a threat with ball in hand. Leigh Halfpenny was nailing everything. So, it was that I and thousands of Lions fans watched a game appear to slip out of our hands. The Lions were being pinged all the time and it inevitably led to a penalty for Beale right in front of the sticks with the score at 23 – 21 to the Lions. My nerves were shredded it was awful but perversely wonderful. We all know what happened next and I, as did thousands of others erupted, what a brilliant start to the series. Australia could count themselves a little unlucky, but my god how many games have they won in the last minute, it was our turn. My friend from Quantas came over at the end to say that I was lucky three times over 1. I was on holiday 2. My team had won and 3. I was sitting with the best-looking woman in the bar, I smiled shook hands and didn't tell Lisa! I was now looking forward to the second test, where for the first time in three tours we could see not only a Lions win but a series win to boot. In the meantime, we had plenty of travelling to do.

Breakfast at our hotel had been very good. There had been some scares with who was picking us up, but a bloke gave up his Sunday morning to pick us up as there had been a bit of a cock up. The hotel did try to charge for some internet that we had not had, but it wasn't a problem, although at times I thought that I was talking a foreign language. Today we were to embark on the Indian Pacific train to travel to Adelaide.

The Indian Pacific is an Australian passenger rail service running between Sydney and Perth. It is one of the few truly transcontinental trains in the world. The train first ran in February 1970 after the completion of gauge conversion projects in South and Western Australia.

The route includes the world's longest straight stretch of railway track, a 478-kilometre (297 mi) stretch over the Nullarbor Plain. In 1983 the service was extended to serve Adelaide. A one-way trip originally took 75 hours, but with line and efficiency improvements it now takes 65 hours. The train currently has four classes, branded as Platinum, Gold Service and Red

Service Sleeper and Red Service Daynighter and also a Motorail service to convey passengers' motor vehicles.

We had been upgraded from Red Service Sleeper to Gold. Food and drinks were included so another bonus. The train is huge, probably needs to be as they put cars on it as well. Check in was very good and before we knew it we were shown to our cabin by Justin who would look after us. The cabin was very good, with en suite and a radio, the en suite worked very well.

We had travelled by train in India in 2012, from New Delhi to Agra from there to Varanasi, from there to New Jalpaiguri and from there to Kolkata. That was an experience especially in second class where there were six beds along the side of the carriage, and four, four person semi cabins. One journey took us seventeen hours, and as we were white and Lisa blonde we always attracted a lot of quizzical attention. One of the things that happened was that the papers from food would be just thrown into the corridor, so you would have to tip toe over a mess to get to the toilets which after a few hours were carnage. The trains would stop in the middle of nowhere and beggars would get on, together with locals selling chai, which was always very nice in fairness. We did have first class on one trip and that cabin was very like the Indian Pacific without the en suite, inclusive food and drinks! Nevertheless, a brilliant experience, India is a wonderful country.

Back to Perth once we got on I went to explore and found the bar/restaurant car, so as we slowly moved out of Perth we sat and had a couple of glasses of wine before lunch. The car is set up for people to have a chat, we are the type of holiday makers who like to keep ourselves to ourselves but it wasn't really a problem, as we can chat with the best of them. I think that the average age on the train was about 90, however it was ninety years of worldly experience which we would discover.. One poor gent sort of fell over as the train rolled, his reward was a scowl from his wife, like he meant it! Our lunch partners were John and Nancy from Hamilton and for dinner it was John and Leanne from Perth. John from Perth did wedding photographs and showed us some of his photos which were very good. He was Italian by extraction and recommended Lygone Street in Melbourne as a place to go and eat. They were a nice couple. The food was very good and we spent the afternoon and evening passing miles of not a lot, but did see a lot of wild kangaroo. We also dozed a bit it had been an early start and we had drunk a bit of wine, it is a very nice way to pass the time. Later that night we stopped at a place called Kalgoorlie;

In January 1893, prospectors Patrick (Paddy) Hannan, Tom Flanagan, and Dan O'Shea were travelling to Mount Youle when one of their horses cast a shoe. During the halt in their journey, the men noticed signs of gold in the area, and decided to stay and investigate. On 17 June 1893, Hannan filed a Reward

Claim, leading to hundreds of men swarming to the area in search of gold and Kalgoorlie, originally called Hannan's, was born.

The population of the town was 2,018 (1516 males and 502 females) in 1898.

The mining of gold, along with other metals such as nickel, has been a major industry in Kalgoorlie ever since, and today employs about one-quarter of Kalgoorlie's workforce and generates a significant proportion of its income. The concentrated area of large gold mines surrounding the original Hannan find is often referred to as the Golden Mile, and is considered by some to be the richest square mile of earth on the planet. The town's population was about 30,000 people in 1903 and began to grow into nearby Boulder.

In 1901 the population of Kalgoorlie was 4,793 (3087 males and 1706 females) which increased to 6,790 (3904 males and 2886 females).

The narrow gauge Government railway line reached Kalgoorlie in 1896, and the main named railway service from Perth was the overnight sleeper train The Westland which ran until the 1970s. In 1917, a standard gauge railway line was completed, connecting Kalgoorlie to the city of Port Augusta, South Australia across 2,000 kilometres (1,243 mi) of desert, and consequently the rest of the eastern states. The standardisation of the railway connecting Perth (which changed route from the narrow gauge route) in 1968 completed the Sydney-Perth railway, making it possible for rail travel from Perth to Sydney—and the Indian Pacific rail service commenced soon after. During the 1890s, the Goldfields area boomed as a whole, with an area population exceeding 200,000, mainly prospectors. The area gained a notorious reputation for being a wild west with bandits and prostitutes. This rapid increase in population and claims of neglect by the state government in Perth led to the proposition of the new state of Auralia but with the sudden diaspora after the Gold Rush these plans fell through.

Places, famous or infamous, that Kalgoorlie is noted for include its water pipeline, designed by C. Y. O'Connor and bringing in fresh water from Mundaring Weir near Perth, its Hay Street brothels, its two-up school, the goldfields railway loopline, the Kalgoorlie Town Hall, the Paddy Hannan statue/drinking fountain, the Super Pit and Mount Charlotte lookout. Its main street is Hannan Street, named after the town's founder. One of the infamous brothels also serves as a museum and is a major national attraction.

Kalgoorlie and the surrounding district was serviced by an extensive collection of suburban railways and tramways, providing for both passenger and freight traffic.

I wished we could have stayed a bit longer it looked really interesting, the Super Pit and some of its vehicles needed to be seen to be believed. But it was back to the train and bed.

The next morning we ate breakfast with Agnes who was originally from Holland but was married to the man who arranged all of the dining match ups, our maître d' whose name I am afraid escapes me. Agnes made several trips with him every year. I didn't eat much breakfast but it looked good again. The morning saw us make our final stop before Adelaide, Cook.

Cook is a railway station and crossing loop on the standard gauge Trans-Australian Railway from Port Augusta to Kalgoorlie, with no inhabited places around.

The former town was created in 1917 when the railway was built and is named after the sixth Prime Minister of Australia, Joseph Cook. The town depended on the Tea and Sugar Train for the delivery of supplies, and is on the longest stretch of straight railway in the world, at 478 kilometres (297 mi) which stretches from Ooldea to beyond Loongana. When the town was active, water was pumped from an underground Artesian aquifer but now, all water is carried in by train.

The town was effectively closed in 1997 when the railways were privatised and the new owners did not need a support town there. Cook is the only scheduled stop on the Nullarbor Plain for the Indian Pacific passenger train across Australia and has little other than curiosity value for the passengers. The bush hospital is closed, the hospital advertised itself at the station with the catch cry "If you're crook come to Cook". Presumably in an effort to drum up patients, who never appeared.

At lunch we met Jack and Glenys from Melbourne a lovely couple who had travelled plenty. Amongst other trips they had sailed from Fremantle to Harwich, travelled to Hawaii and train wise had done the Melbourne > Adelaide > Alice Springs > Darwin trip. So engrossed was I in their adventures that I can't remember what we ate, although I did have barramundi. The afternoon was spent lounging about in the lounge and dozing in the room, and perhaps the best was kept for last as at dinner we sat with Joe and Joy from the Northern Territories. Joe I have to describe, he was a little rotund, about five foot eight inches tall, wearing a fishing cap, with wild grey hair and an even wilder beard, a smile never left his face, they were great company. Joy had been a nurse, Joe 'fished and cut grass' he was also a Vietnam veteran,

The Vietnam War was the longest major conflict in which Australians have been involved; it lasted ten years, from 1962 to 1972, and involved some 60,000 personnel. A limited initial commitment of just 30 military advisers grew to include a battalion in 1965 and finally, in 1966, a task force. Each of the three services was involved, but the dominant role was played by the Army.

In the early years, Australia's participation in the war was not widely opposed. But as the commitment grew, as conscripts began to make up a large percentage of those being deployed and killed, and as the public increasingly came to believe that the war was being lost, opposition grew until, in the early 1970s, more than 200,000 people marched in the streets of Australia's major cities in protest.

By this time the United States Government had embarked on a policy of 'Vietnamisation' - withdrawing its own troops from the country while passing responsibility for the prosecution and conduct of the war to South Vietnamese forces. Australia too was winding down its commitment and the last combat troops came home in March 1972. The RAAF, however, sent personnel back to Vietnam in 1975 to assist in evacuations and humanitarian work during the war's final days. Involvement in the war cost more than 500 Australian servicemen their lives, while some 3,000 were wounded, otherwise injured or were victims of illness.

For Australia, the Vietnam War was the cause of the greatest social and political dissent since the conscription referenda of the First World War.

Of all the things we spoke about what intrigued me was the wildlife that appears to be accessible to all homeowners in Australia, in Joe and Joy's case the Big Brown snake;

The brown snake is approximately 1.5 metres long, and is one of Australia's more deadly creatures. They have venom which can cause death to humans relatively quickly if left untreated. Brown snakes up to 2.3 metres have been recorded in Australia.

They feed on small creatures, such as mice and rats, small birds, lizards or even other snakes.

they had once found one in their sunroom.

The Indian Pacific had been a good idea and we were glad that we had done it, the staff……...apart from one had been great so thanks to Nada and Justin if you ever read this and get some customer service skills to the bloke behind the bar.

We arrived in Adelaide quite early in the morning and were picked up straight away and dropped at our hotel, the Majestic Rooftop. Straight into the room which was good, and that allowed us to have a good walk around Adelaide. We headed first for the Adelaide Oval firstly crossing the Torrens river where Australia showed its wildlife diversity as we walked past pelicans in the park.

The River Torrens is the most significant river of the Adelaide Plains and was one of the reasons for the citing of the city of Adelaide. The upper stretches of the river and the reservoirs in its watershed supply a significant part of the city's water. .

At its 1836 discovery an inland bend was chosen as the site of the Adelaide city centre and North Adelaide. The river is named after Colonel Robert Torrens, chairman of the colonial commissioners and a significant figure in the city's founding. The river is also known by its native Kaurna name Karra wirra-parri.

During the early years of settlement, the river acted as both the city's primary water source and main sewer, leading to outbreaks of typhus and cholera.

I had really looked forward to seeing the Oval, sadly its was being re-constructed and looked nothing like the Victorian gem that I had seen and held in my memory banks. We walked all the way around and did notice that some of the old buildings were still there, I was however overall disappointed. We continued on our walk into the city, which was again easy to walk around, and had a light PIE lunch at a street side café. Got to give it to the Aussies they can make a pie. After this we carried on into the shopping centre and down to the central market.

On Saturday, 23rd January 1869 at 3.15am a group of market gardeners made their way to a site between Gouger and Grote Street and started to sell their produce. The official opening of the Adelaide Central Market was on the 22nd January 1870. On the 8th February 1900, the first stone was laid to build the current Central Market façade, which still stands today. In the same year, a 40-meter veranda was added. Gas lighting, which had been sufficient for almost 35 years was replaced by electricity in March, 1902. Early in the morning of 27th December 1925 the market in the north-eastern section suffered fire damage. The fire brigade managed to restrict damage to two shops. The Central

Market was officially named in August 1965, prior to this the market was known as the City Market. On the night of 27th June 1977, a major portion of the southern stall area of the market was badly damaged by fire causing half a million dollars' worth of damage. Refurbishment work began to repair damage caused by fire. Work was completed in 1983.

The Central Market today remains "the Heart of Adelaide".

We were looking for, but couldn't seem to find Coopers Alehouse, so we decided to head back to the hotel for a rest. As there was the Lions game against the Melbourne Rebels on TV that night I decided to head back out to find the alehouse, found it and confirmed not only that the match was on, but also that there was a happy hour and they did food. A result, there was a bit of a police incident on the way back to the hotel, but despite all the noise and sirens I could not see what was going on.

We left the hotel to make good use of the happy hour at Coopers Alehouse, and had a nice few drinks before the game. During the game, there were other Lions supporters in the bar and after going to the toilet I had a brief chat with a couple who were both Scottish, Sandy and Norrie. I asked them if they had been to the first test, they said that they had, and had been lucky getting tickets, as on the day standing tickets had become available. Chris Brierley had text me to say that someone in Melbourne was after tickets and that I could sell my spares quite easily. However, as I had two Lions fans in front of me I asked Sandy and Norrie if they had tickets for the game, they said not, so I told them that I had two standing if they wanted them, and that they could have them for what they cost me A$175. They were over the moon you would have thought that I was Father Christmas. They wanted to pay me there and then, but I said that I wouldn't take any money until I had the tickets, which would not be until the following day. They were leaving Adelaide early so we gave them Lisa's mobile number and agreed to meet up in Melbourne once we had arrived. They were so pleased that they wanted to buy us drinks all night and our dinner, I agreed to one and to make sure there were no more kept going to the other end of the bar to get served and order food. They were a great couple of blokes but I was just happy we had got the tickets to some real fans. The match ended 35 v 0 to the Lions a comfortable win. For dinner, we decided on another Australian staple the Snitty or Schnitzel to you and I. There was a choice of sixteen ounces or twenty-four ounces, I am glad we went for the former, as that was huge, especially with the sauce, I had mushroom, and Lisa black pepper, very good and very filling. After food we said good bye to Sandy and Norrie and walked back to the hotel, not a bad evening at all.

The next day Dan picked us up bright and early from the hotel, there were of course two important exchanges to be made. Two packs of ReadyBrek for Dan and the

Lions tickets for us, formalities completed we headed off to McClaren Vale where he lived and where he was going to show us some vineyards. Noticeable was the mix of Dan's potteries accent with some Australian twang. He told us that one of his first jobs as a Police Officer in Adelaide had been to check if there was actually a White Shark in one of the bays, a tough one that. He also told us about the summer heat, difficulties with bush fires and his progress in South Australia since he left the UK six years before. He was doing well and had taken up cycling as a hobby. Our first stop was in his home town where we had coffee and met his partner Carla, a New Zealander who had lived in the UK for a while. Then it was off to the Coriole vineyard to taste some wine.

Coriole is situated in the undulating hills of the densely planted <u>McLaren Vale</u> region just within sight of the sea and less than an hour from Adelaide.

The original farmhouses were built in 1860 and are now the epicentre of the garden and cellar door at the winery. The original vineyards were planted immediately after the first world war.

Shiraz is the great tradition of McLaren Vale going back over 150 years, and is the major variety planted on the estate. The first wine released was the 1970 Claret (Shiraz). Coriole has been an Australian pioneer of Sangiovese and Italian varieties since 1985.

Coriole is managed by two family members, Mark and Paul Lloyd.

The weather was glorious, blue sky and a temperature like a good late spring day at home, the vineyard had great views across the hills, it was a nice setting. Better still as we walked in a friend of Dan and Carla said 'we have just opened an 89 chardonnay do you want some' we needed no encouragement. We spent the next couple of hours shooting the breeze and drinking some lovely wine. In fact it was here that Lisa got a taste for red wine Temperanillo reeling her in.

From here we went to Ekhidna for lunch.

EKHIDNA (or Echidna) was a monstrous she-dragon (drakaina) with the head and breast of a woman. She probably represented or presided over the corruptions of the earth: rot, slime, fetid waters, illness and disease.

She was often equated with Python (the rotting one), a dragon born of the fetid slime left behind by the great Deluge. Others call her the Tartarean lamprey, and assigned her to the dark, swampy pit of Tartaros beneath the earth. Hesiod, makes her a daughter of monstrous sea-gods, and presumably associates her with rotting sea-scum and fetid salt-marshes.

In all cases, she was described as the consort of Typhoeus, a monstrous storm-daemon who challenged Zeus in heaven. Together they spawned a host of terrible monsters to plague the earth.

Other closely related she-dragons included the Argive Ekhidna and Poine, the Tartarean Kampe, and the Phokian Sybaris.

The restaurant was very good. It had wines from the region and some local real ale which to be honest were a bit sparse in Australia apart perhaps from Cooper's. Lisa had moussaka, Dan, Carla and I shared a platter of chorizo, ham, artichokes and different breads, it was a very pleasant way to spend lunch, which had to be our treat. Soon we were off again to another winery, and a little more tasting, we benefitted from Carla driving as it was now latish afternoon. We then popped into Dan and Carla's abode and made our way back into town for dinner. On our walk the day before we had come across a 'lively' part of Adelaide, which is where we headed for now, to eat at Apothecary 1878. The restaurant is actually situated in the more racey part of town but the locals are friendly. It is a lovely old building with some of the old chemist things still on display. There is a room downstairs for private functions. We had a starter to share, our chicken thighs were a little bit overdone but they were okay. I had the belly pork as a main and would have preferred it in strips rather than chopped up because the dish looked like and was a little like couscous with the pork in it. It tasted nice and the wine was good, as was the company. Carla was amongst other things a nutritionist and sold us on the benefits of pro biotics, the next day we bought some and posted it on Facebook which had Dan commenting about how he would now have to do it. Well it might assist his 100-mile cycle rides! After dinner despite the offers we decided to walk back to the hotel with our wines from the region, just to get some exercise in an otherwise gorging day. Which had been a great one thanks to our hosts Dan and Carla. Dan having also supplied a nice foam crate for our wines and the flight home. Safely back at the billet, sleep was not very far behind.

After an early start the chemist and pro biotics was the first call, followed by dragging the cases on a short walk to where we could collect our hire car. No problems with the booking there were problems with the car, mainly me. The car was an automatic and I couldn't get it going or out of the garage without a lot of assistance and then we were off, well not actually. The Sat Nav taking us in an opposite direction to where we wanted to head which was basically south of Adelaide. We wanted to go to Raglan Road 400 miles away, there is a Raglan Road in Adelaide. It does help however if you put the right state into the Sat Nav and then after wandering round Adelaide in circles for a bit we were really on our way south. Again, the weather was good for a drive and we did for a couple of hours until we pulled into the tiny town of Coonapil, so tiny I can find no other reference to it, but it did have a post office that was advertising PIES. We went to investigate and despite the complete lack of customer service skills demonstrated by the lady behind the counter we opted for a beef and onion and a beef and cheese. Crispy pastry, nice filling, you know the score utterly gorgeous and on we went. The Sat Nav was showing a bit of a daft arrival time until we realised that we were heading towards a half an hour time zone once we got into Victoria despite the fact we were still probably due south from Adelaide. Our next stop just as it was going dark was Portland, here we found a little café that did some great coffee and also some Dim Sum which we had to try. The lady in here did great customer service and was really very friendly. Sadly, the day before they had the Southern Right Whale in the bay so we had just missed them. We didn't really have a lot of time to stop so we carried on. We had hoped to see Kangaroos on the journey, sadly we did but they were all dead at the side of the road. I wouldn't like to have seen the cars, they hit, some of them were huge. At 6.20pm after a very long drive we got to our hotel the Comfort Inn on Raglan in Warrnambool;

The word Warrnambool originates from the local Indigenous Australians name for a nearby volcanic cone. It is interpreted to mean many things including land between two rivers, two swamps or ample water.

A popular legend is that the first Europeans to discover Warrnambool were Cristóvão de Mendonça and his crew who surveyed the coastline nearby and were marooned near the site of the present town as early as the 16th century, based on the unverified reports of local whaler's discovery of the wreck of a mahogany ship. The ship's provenance has been variously attributed to France, China, Spain and Portugal. There is no physical evidence to suggest that it ever existed.

The Lady Nelson under Lieutenant James Grant sailed along the coast in December 1800 and named several features, followed by Matthew Flinders in the Investigator and French explorer Nicholas Baudin, who recorded coastal landmarks, in 1802. The area was frequented by whalers early in the 19th century.

The first settlers arrived in the 1840s in the Lady Bay area, which was a natural harbour. The town was surveyed in 1846 and established soon after, the Post Office opening on 1 January 1849.

During the Victorian Gold Rush, Warrnambool became an important port and grew quickly in the 1850s, benefiting from the private ownership of nearby Port Fairy. It was gazetted as a municipality in 1855, and became a borough in 1863. Warrnambool was declared a town in 1883, and a city in 1918.

We were clearly now on a role customer service wise as the lady at the hotel, Ann was brilliant, very helpful getting us settled, showing us how to use the air conditioning and pointing out where town was. She was even interested in the spelling of my name;

***"Ian"**, **"Iain"** (/ˈiː.ən/; Scottish Gaelic pronunciation: [ˈɪʲən]) is a name of Gaelic origin, corresponding to English John. It is a very common name in much of the English-speaking world and especially in Scotland, where it originated.*

A twenty-minute walk into town it was, which gave the legs a good shake and we stumbled on the Seanchai Irish pub, with an open fire and welcoming staff so had a couple there. It was relatively late, not many places were open so we went up to the Victoria Hotel for a drink, they were doing food but we had seen a noodle takeaway and decided to go for that after a couple more. Up by the hotel was a 24-hour Drive In. Yes drive in bottle shop, or off licence to some of us. Had to be seen to be believed. Just pull in with your truck and twenty-four cans later you are away, we got and carried a couple of bottles. The noodles were great so the choice had been good, a doze in front of the TV and that was us happy and content with our quick visit to Warrnambool.

The next morning saw us start the drive down the great Ocean road, where we looked at the twelve apostles, well eight actually due to erosion.

The apostles were formed by erosion: the harsh and extreme weather conditions from the Southern Ocean gradually eroded the soft limestone to form caves in the cliffs, which then became arches, which in turn collapsed; leaving rock stacks up to 45 metres high. Now because of this erosion there are less than ten remaining. The site was known as the Sow and Piglets until 1922 after which it was renamed to The Apostles for tourism purposes. The formation eventually became known as the Twelve Apostles, despite only ever having nine stacks.

The stacks are susceptible to further erosion from the waves. On 3 July 2005, a 50-metre-tall stack collapsed, leaving eight remaining. On 25 September 2009, it was thought that another of the stacks had fallen, but this was actually one of the smaller stacks of the Three Sisters formation. The rate of erosion at the base of the limestone pillars is approximately 2 cm per year. Due to wave action eroding the cliff face existing headlands are expected to become new limestone stacks in the future.

It would be fair to say that you don't actually drive along the Ocean, you drive adjacent to it then pull into a number of viewing points as you move along. One of these was the scene of the shipwreck of a ship called Loch Ard.

The Loch Ard departed England on 1 March 1878, bound for Melbourne, commanded by Captain Gibb and with a crew of 17 men. It was carrying 37 passengers and assorted cargo. On 1 June, the ship was approaching Melbourne and expecting to sight land when it encountered heavy fog. Unable to see the Cape Otway lighthouse, the captain was unaware how close he was running to the coast. The fog lifted around 4am, revealing breakers and cliff faces. Captain Gibb quickly ordered sail to be set to come about and get clear of the coast, but they were unable to do so in time, and ran aground on a reef. The masts and rigging came crashing down, killing some people on deck and preventing the lifeboats from being launched effectively. The ship sank within 10 or 15 minutes of striking the reef.

The only two survivors of the wreck were Eva Carmichael, who survived by clinging to a spar for five hours, and Thomas (Tom) R. Pearce, an apprentice who clung to the overturned hull of a lifeboat. Tom Pearce came ashore first, then heard Eva's shouts and went back into the ocean to rescue her. They came ashore at what is now known as Loch Ard Gorge and sheltered there before seeking assistance. The Loch Ard's cargo included a range of luxury goods, including a large decorative porcelain peacock made by Minton in England, intended to be displayed in the Melbourne International Exhibition in 1880.

Having spent a nice couple of hours seeing the sights along the coast we headed towards Melbourne stopping off at a bakery in Coloc on the way. Our accommodation 'Robinsons in the city' was easily found and we dropped off our stuff before then dropping the hire car off. My next task was to get the tickets to Sandy and Norrie as we had been exchanging texts and agreed to meet at the Park Hyatt. I gave myself twenty minutes to get there but did not realise it was the other side of town, so panicking I started to run, got to the front door and could not see anyone. I didn't have a phone so was running blind, so to speak, what did we ever do before we got mobile phones? Once in the hotel I checked I had come in the front and was relieved to be told I hadn't and shown the front door. Outside was Sandy who was as relieved to see me as I was him, I gave him the tickets, he gave me a bear hug, I am not small five foot ten and fourteen stone, but I was swamped by his mass! He gave me Aus$250 to which I told him that was too much as I only wanted the Aus$175 that I had paid, he insisted, we shook hands and off he went. Nice couple of blokes but I was more than pleased to get two more Lions fans into the Etihad. I nipped for a quick drink on the way back to our digs and then we went for a walk into town. We decided to follow the advice from John on the train and after going into the Sherlock Holmes bar went up to Lygone Street. Here we found a bustling restaurant area and La Spaghetteria where my parmigiana and Lisa's lasagne did the trick. Lions fans were as usual, everywhere. We text Graham Hughes to meet up the next night and it was back to the room. I spent a short time in the lounge just before turning in, some other guests arrived. Our host introduced me to them as 'our model guest' and they had even stuck a Lions shirt on me to make the guests feel at home! Nice humour, nice bloke, nice establishment.

Wallabies versus the British and Irish Lions, Saturday 29th June 2013 Etihad Stadium, Melbourne

At breakfast the next day it turned out the couple from the night before were from Brisbane, the lady's sister lived in Wheelock, which is about two miles from where I live, a small world. Breakfast was taken at a large table with the other guests, most of whom were going to the game. Subterfuge had been used to get tickets, one lady even getting an Australian SIM card so she could give an Australian mobile number. Today of course was match day and I was over excited already. We decided to have a stroll to the stadium which was a short walk away. There we met a bloke in a Lions two-piece suit as we took pictures with Chris's Liverpool duck. He said that there must be a story attached we told him the story and he insisted the duck be photographed with him, which it was. We then had a stroll around the local market before it was back to the room to change into the match kit. For me the 2005 top which I had worn in Pretoria and also when seeing the Lions win in Johannesburg and Brisbane on TV. Lisa had the white 2009 version. It was still hours before the game but the atmosphere was building.

So out we stepped with a series win a very big possibility, as is usual there were red shirts everywhere and we decided to walk to the other side of town then to come back on ourselves. There were a lot of gold shirts as well. There were also a lot of celebrities around just before the first pub we saw Mark Taylor the Australian cricketer and former captain, missed that photo opportunity but a better one was to follow. As we walked down the road towards the Duke of Wellington pub, walking towards us was none other than a proper

Lions legend Doctor James Robson, who as you will know has been on a number of Lions tours.

'Any chance of a picture Dr Robson', he looked a bit surprised but said no problem at all, so we had our photograph taken by one of his physio team, great stuff nice man and nice people all round. Pleased as punch we walked off into the pub. In the way were ex Wallabies Justin Harrison, Joe Roff and Chris Larkham! I walked around them and we had a nice few drinks in the bar. We needed to eat, everywhere was packed so we dropped into possibly the worst McDonalds in the history of that company, it was awful, dirty, dirty toilets you name it they had it and yes, the food was rank as well, bad call. Putting that quickly behind us we went up to the team hotel the Grand Hyatt. It was by now about two hours to kick off and the bus was outside, we had a quick drink in the bar then waited for the team to come out with hundreds of others. We waited and we waited and we waited. I was seriously concerned that they would be in a rush. I needn't have worried as when the boys came out they had their game face on, there was no smiling or waving to the throngs so we cheered them onto the bus and made our own way to the ground.

The roof was on at the stadium, the atmosphere just brilliant, and beers under the seat we awaited history. The people to my right were Australians, to our left an Irish bloke. It was awash with red and gold, but what support for the Lions, incredible when you think that the majority had come from the UK. The Australian anthem was countered by bread of heaven and we were off. The Lions started the game like they meant business, with Captain Sam going for the corner after an early penalty miss, that didn't come to anything try wise but another penalty gave the Lions the lead. The first twenty minutes were spent in the gold half of the pitch. After this it became a classic war of attrition Test match. The hits were brutal no one would take a backward step and penalties were the only scores with Lealifano kicking everything, Leigh wasn't too dusty either. 12 – 9 at half time and as I write this I can still feel the butterflies of what inevitably was becoming a tense affair with everything to play for, it was quite wonderful sporting entertainment and the crowd were loving it. We nipped to meet Chris Brierley at the interval, and, as is his norm gave us four tickets for the 'Lions Den' after the match.

So back to the rugby which really was of a high quality with defences at the fore. There was of course the now famous George North versus Folau moment where giant George picked him up and drove him back to a huge roar of approval from the Lions fans. On sixty-two minutes the Lions took a 15 – 9 lead after a penalty won at the scrum. There now started what I can only call a golden rage, the Australians striving desperately to take the match, the Lions not for moving. Critically Captain Sam, who Clive Woodward said had played one of the best matches ever by an open side, left the field with a torn hamstring, you could practically see it tearing on the replay, what a game he had. But now the gold rush became more intense, it was nail biting stuff and utterly compelling. The Lions were not for moving and glancing at the clock with five minutes to go I screamed:

'defend for our lives boys, defend for our lives' to which my Irish friend said

'I hate six point leads'

Sadly and inevitably, given the pressure the Lions brave line cracked briefly and Adam Ashley Cooper crossed for a try. Lealifano kicked a brilliant conversion and the Lions trailed by a point. Given how much we had been on the back foot, was there still time for a score? The Lions went for it, and after a very rare mistake by Genia they had a line out deep in our half, which we had to win and had to then get up the pitch. The line out was won the ball sent down the line, the hooter went, signifying that time was up, it was edge of the seat stuff it really was. George North gave a brilliant pass out of nothing and the Lions crept to the halfway line. Then it happened, penalty to the Lions right underneath where we sat. It was a long way out:

'This is it this is it!' I screamed to my fellow supporters, I am in tears now, I was then it couldn't be could it, we win in the dying moments not the green and gold?

Leigh Halfpenny stepped up, it looked in his range, my mind flashed back to that kick in the RWC 2011 semi-final, this was longer. I along with many others could barely look, but I did, up the kick flew making ground initially……but then stalling and falling short, the Lions despite a supreme effort had been beaten. As in Pretoria I was gutted, I looked at the pitch, Leigh was inconsolable, James Horwill was in tears it meant that much. Regardless of the result I was proud of our team they were phenomenal. There was nothing left to do but leave the ground……. gutted.

Graham and Jill were outside to meet us and we went into the 'Lions Den' to meet Chris, despite the result it was a good atmosphere albeit the beer was expensive but the food very welcome. The band were not too bad either and we also got to meet Andy Nichol the Scottish scrum half who had a quick word with Graham. He had almost played for the Lions in 2001 when called into the squad whilst on holiday due to a squad crisis. The hours flew but at 1am we called it a day and walked back to our billet with Graham and Jill carrying on to theirs.

Chapter 24
On the way home

You know when you wake up and remember something almost immediately that puts you down in the dumps? Well that was the feeling that I had the next morning, our last day in Australia. I was still gutted and still upset and still sad, but we had a day to enjoy so it was up and at them. Talk at the breakfast table, was of course about the game, but we couldn't change the result. A big walk beckoned for me and Lisa.

We commenced by walking to Yarra Park, en route we went down Gertrude Street which looked very bohemian and I wished we would have had time to see it, at night time. We decided we needed one more pie so walked past the MCG and Australian Tennis site to go and get one, they didn't disappoint. Neither did the MCG a magnificent sight, filling up nicely for an Aussie rules game. The weather that day was really not bad at all. So we kept walking and found ourselves eventually at the Limerick Arms hotel on Clarendon Street, we had walked miles, overall that day it would be eighteen. We also went into the Waterside on Flinders Street where the bar man told us:

'I didn't realise how much beer the Lions would drink we have run out of nearly everything!'

Because you see dear reader for Lions read players, staff and fans it's the whole picture and that is what makes it so special.

A few drinks saw us stop off at the Rice Paper on Swanston Street where we had chicken rolls, char siu chicken, beef satay and best of all, soft shell crab, that was gorgeous. That left us with time for a couple more drinks with Graham and Jill, who were going onto Sydney, at the Sherlock Holmes and it was back to the billet.

Our pick up the next morning was bang on time and we breezed through check in and security to very quickly be looking at our Airbus. And we looked and we looked until on seeing a lot of staff at the gate I said to Lisa:

'This doesn't look good'

And it wasn't; our plane was broken and they were going to have to fly one in so instead of landing at Heathrow Tuesday morning at 5.30am it would be Tuesday night at 7.30pm. Some people would say that another night in Australia at no cost would be a result, not if you want to go home it isn't, and not if it takes hours to get your bags back. In the darkness we arrived at a Rydges Hotel, where we had a nice meal, the staff were great and the room was fine. A 3am call and we were back to the airport where it took us hours to book in. We did get the leg room seats that we paid for. There was also time to take in that Gatland had gone for ten Welshmen in the final test team. The god that is BOD had been dropped in favour of the Wales centre pairing. To be honest some of the comments leading up to the game, in particular from Keith Wood and, dare I say it, Willie John McBride were really far from helpful:

Willie John McBride expects Australia coach Robbie Deans will be delighted after the British and Irish Lions omitted Brian O'Driscoll from Saturday's decisive third Test in Sydney.

O'Driscoll has been sensationally dropped from the Lions Test squad altogether as Warren Gatland rolls the dice for the must-win series decider against Australia in Sydney by making six changes.

The four-time tourist, widely considered to be the finest player of his generation, was the favourite to captain the Lions in what would have been his final game in the iconic red jersey after Sam Warburton was ruled out with a grade-one hamstring tear.

McBride told BBC Radio 4: 'I was absolutely gutted. The first thing that came into my mind was that Deans, the Australian coach, must be laughing all the way.

'The Australian media and others, Eddie Jones the previous Australian coach, have convinced them to drop O'Driscoll which I find amazing.

Willie had wanted BOD as captain so I suppose it was inevitable.

Former Lions and Ireland forward Keith Wood said that, in the absence of Paul O'Connell, the Lions should have retained O'Driscoll for his experience alone. Wood accused Gatland of devaluing the Lions captaincy by failing to appreciate its significance.

Wood said: "I've been uncomfortable throughout this tour whenever Warren Gatland has spoken about the captaincy. He tries to depower it, he consistently says it isn't about leadership and that isn't the most important thing. Having been on two Lions tours myself under [former England captain] Martin Johnson, I would have said the leadership of the captain was the most important thing.

"Brian O'Driscoll has been quiet in the two Tests but at every stage he has been the clarion call once Paul O'Connell got injured. Gatland has made a terrible mistake."

Both as rugby icons are entitled to their opinion but it was not helpful in the build up to a series decider, the legendary JPR said that there should have been more Welshmen! The bottom line was that they were not Welshmen they were Lions it is and was as simple as that. I thought that the comments were myopic, and think that Keith Wood has been anti Welsh ever since.

Back to the airport and we took off fifteen minutes late but had a pleasant flight to Dubai including going over Uluru which had a special significance for Lisa and I. On this part of the flight the man next to me by the exit door said that his wife was in business and that they were going to let him go up to see here, we didn't see him on the second leg of the flight, lucky him? Having leg room is great the one drawback is with all the room, people come up to stretch their legs. Some use it like Muscle Beach, some of the exercises need to be seen to be believed they are ludicrous and usually done by people who look like they have never exercised in their life. It can also be very very funny. Heathrow was found in the dark and it wasn't very long before we experienced one of the sad selfish traits of everyday life.

We got to the stop to get a lift for the car first, we were then joined by a number of people. When the mini bus came, the driver started filling it from the back of the queue. This left us as the last to get on, there were no seats, everyone on the bus knew we were first and the driver refused to go with people standing up. Due to the impasse I said we would get off and in stony silence thanked everyone else on the bus for taking their turn in the queue I didn't get an answer, pure selfishness nothing else. The journey home saw Lisa driving first with me doing everything to keep us awake, window open, radio on, talking rubbish. We swapped over at Birmingham, I was hoping for more of the same from Lisa, I looked after about five minutes driving to see, she was fast asleep! We got home safely at about 1.30am on the Wednesday and did have a very good sleep.

The tale of our tours is nearly finished, there was however the 3rd test to witness, even if it was on TV. The Saturday morning had me planning a game of golf followed by the game at home. The golf done I ran across the car park and got home with five minutes gone but with the game being recorded so I witnessed the great start late, the start was great, wasn't it? But as they do the Aussies got back into it before half time and it was worrying. I won't now dwell on the point but in the second half the Lions were brilliant and destroyed the Aussies for a great series win, I wish I had been there, but my TV 'lucky' New Zealand 2005 shirt had come through again.

So there it is eight years in the making, we hadn't seen the Lions win live but we had been part of the supporting cast. It had been a great experience and we had loved every minute, we had seen some great places and met some lovely people, and written a book to boot.

Will we go again? Well we have yet to see the Lions win live, so we might take in a midweek game in 2017, see you there.

Travel Lions – Supplement, New Zealand 2017

We went in the end, we had to do really. Five days in New Zealand in 2005 just couldn't justify a brilliant country.

It will come as no surprise to those who have read Travel Lions that tickets were once again a source of complete frustration. Once more the only way to get 'official' tickets was by, purchasing a holiday to go with them. As in 2005 Trevor Palin gave it a go in the ballot for us, as did we under his Auckland address. But to no avail. We did however get Hurricanes tickets, again posing as locals. Well that happened initially.

Whilst watching a super 15 game, I saw an advert for hospitality tickets. I looked them up on the internet, and thought we would give it a go. I had a query so emailed the NZ ticket office. Basically I was told that as I had a 'European' email address I couldn't buy the tickets. When I queried why not, I was told that we have to go through the 'Official Lions' agents. Please see above. When I pointed out the issues I was still told I couldn't have the tickets.

So effectively I had been stopped buying advertised tickets because of who I was. I complained to the New Zealand Human Rights Commission. In fairness they investigated but disagreed with me. I think they were wrong, do you?

The story doesn't end there. Having got the Hurricanes tickets, in March we received an email from NZRFU. It said that the ballot was opening again for Test tickets as 'they had now fulfilled the official and corporate requirements'. So we got two for the third test. I n fact despite news to the contrary, tickets for all Lions games were available week commencing 13th March 2017. Amazing really. My view is that this is because of the practice of companies being allowed to snaffle them all up and advertise holiday packages. What should happen is that those fans, who don't want those packages should have access to a queue or a ballot. I am pretty certain many fans will have been put off by the price of 'packages' and given up on going to New Zealand. Now with tickets available it is probably too late.

So we will be there via Kuala Lumpur with Singapore, and a return to Raffles on the way home. In New Zealand we will be going to Hamilton, Wellington, Blenheim, Greymouth, Franz Josef, Queenstown, Dunedin, Christchurch, Cape Kidnapper, Rotorua, Bay of Islands and Auckland. See you there OR hope you enjoyed it all AND we won!